P9-CRA-029

LINCOLN CHRISTIAN COLLEGE AND SEMINARY

A CUP

OF COFFEE

AT THE

Soul
CAFE

A CUP

OF COFFEE

AT THE

Soul
CAFE

LEONARD SWEET
WITH DENISE MARIE SIINO

BROADMAN
&HOLMAN
PUBLISHERS

Nashville, Tennessee

© 1998
by Leonard I. Sweet
All rights reserved
Printed in the United States of America

0-8054-0159-8

Published by Broadman & Holman Publishers, Nashville, Tennessee
Acquisitions & Development Editor: Leonard Goss
Cover & Inside Page Design: Anderson Thomas Design
Typesetting: TF Designs, Mt. Juliet, Tennessee

Dewey Decimal Classification: 248.1
Subject Heading: Spiritual Life
Library of Congress Card Catalog Number: 97-51742

Unless otherwise stated all Scripture citation is from the Revised Standard Version of the Bible, copyrighted 1946, 1952, © 1971, 1973. Other versions cited are NEB, The New English Bible, © The Delegates of the Oxford University Press and the Syndics of the Cambridge University Press, 1961, 1970, reprinted by permission; NIV, the Holy Bible, New International Version, copyright © 1973, 1978, 1984 by International Bible Society; NKJV, New King James Version, copyright © 1979, 1980, 1982, Thomas Nelson, Inc., Publishers; NRSV, New Revised Standard Version of the Bible, copyright © 1989 by the Division of Christian Education of the National Council of Churches of Christ in the United States of America. Used by permission. All rights reserved.

Library of Congress Cataloging-in-Publication Data
Sweet, Leonard I.
    A cup of coffee at the soul cafe: finding the energy of a deeper spiritual life / Leonard Sweet with Denise Marie Siino.
        p.   cm.
    ISBN 0-8054-0159-8
    1.Spiritual life.
    I. Siino, Denise Marie, 1958- .   II. Title.
BV4501.2.S877   1998
    248.4'861—dc21

97-51742
CIP

3 4 5 02 01 00 99 98

CONTENTS

Prologue   vi

Introduction   1

1   Is Your Clay Moist?   6

2   Onions and Artichokes   17

3   Discipleship = Relationship   28

4   Jesus Wept   37

5   God in Our Midst   47

6   Creation—The Sound (Song) of God   58

7   Prayer: More than a Zen Thing   72

8   Ancient/Future Faith and Hope   82

9   Growing a Soul   93

10 The Fragrance of Integrity   114

11 No Fear!   127

12 The Mystery of Suffering   148

13 Trusting God's Faithfulness   160

14 Spiritual Heirlooms   171

100468

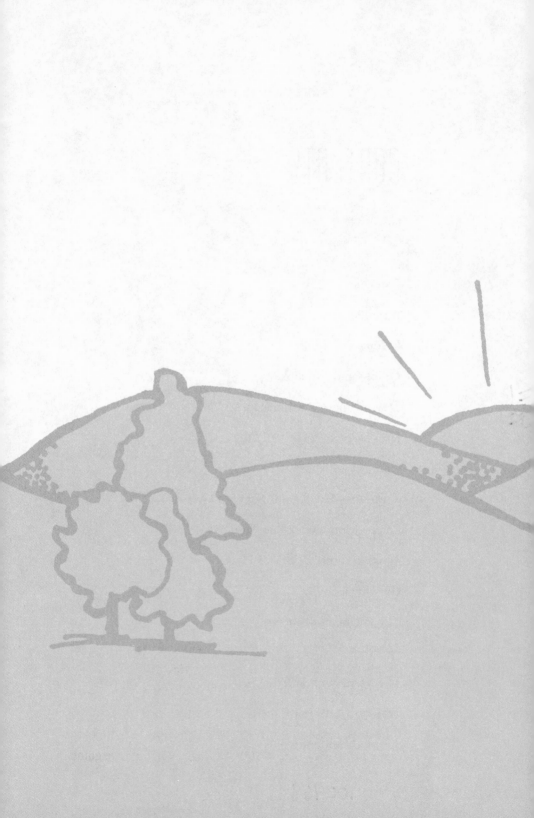

PROLOGUE

If there's anything the generations of the '90s in America share in common these days, it's a recognition that life is not merely a means to an end but a journey—a journey toward finding one's purpose in life. People look in a variety of places for that deeper meaning—power, wealth, meditation, religion. Some never find it. For the disciple of Christ, discovering life's purpose is only in relationship with God, the Creator and Sustainer of life, and in achieving the balance between "inward discovery" and "outward recovery."

Inward discovery refers to a state of being, defining ourselves in terms of who we are in relationship to God as opposed to what we do with our time and energies. Outward recovery refers to our interaction with the world around us, with all its relationships, twists, turns, and monkey wrenches! Sometimes people try to live their lives without first making that spiritual connection, from "the outside in." That's like trying to drive a car with little more than fumes in the gas tank—you probably won't get where you're going and the journey will be hair-raising at best! Living from "the inside out," on the other hand, means living life fully and deliberately, even in the midst of outer turmoil.

To that end, *A Cup of Coffee at the SoulCafe* is a tool for the journey, like a road map on a cross-country trip. Like any good guide, it describes ways to enhance your journey, as well as "sights" you're sure to encounter along the way. Just as you would muse over a road map before taking a trip, this book is best read in meditation and reflection, taking in little bits at a time and chewing on them for a while. Before you get started, let Leonard give you a few rules for the road:

1. You can't steer a parked car. The result of an overactive attention to control and security is stagnation. Only by risking, by opening ourselves to the outside, by trusting, by beginning to move, do we gain the opportunity to participate in a dynamic future.

2. You can't drive forward without a rearview mirror. We must have our past in sight, not as a souvenir, but as a guidepost showing us where we've been and aiding us to where we will be in the future.

3. You can't pass in the slow lane. We must make ample use of our time to make a difference in our world. Those who go slow get left behind.

4. You can't repair the car while it's still in motion. Movement is not an end in itself. When we are exhausted and in need of repair, the worst thing to do is to step on the gas. It is play, repair, and maintenance that give us the creativity to advance.

5. You can't run on empty. Everyone has to have fuel. The fuel we select determines our staying power. Our fuel is the free energy of faith in Jesus Christ.

This book is written in conversational style, in chunks and fragments, like any good, lively discussion. For that's what it is: an active dialogue with Len Sweet, with yourself, with God. Everyone's journey starts in a different place, and though our destination is heaven and our goal is a deeper walk with the Creator, the roads each individual travels will vary. No matter where you begin or what path you take, this book will help you along the way.

—Denise Marie Siino

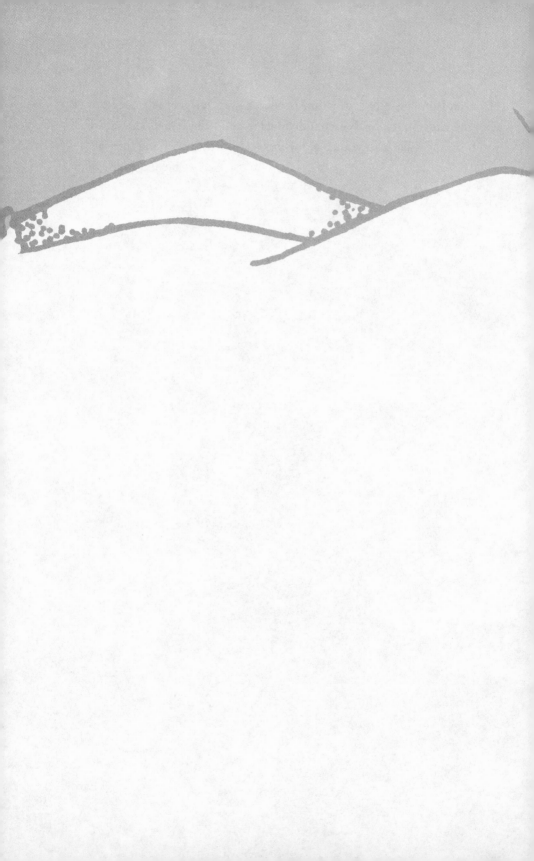

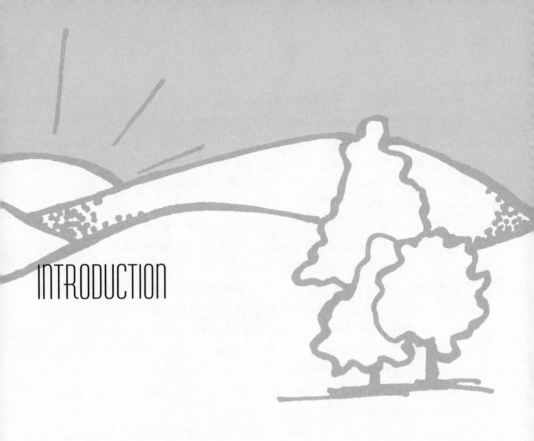

INTRODUCTION

"What in the world is a high-tech store like this doing in such a remote place?" the question invariably goes, as visitors walk into *Sweet's Body & SoulCafe and Mountain Store* for the first time. Then, sure enough, one guest will get absorbed in the soul-food bookshelf while another sits down, cappuccino in hand, before a computer terminal and loses himself in one of the many bookmarked websites, while still another just stands there, soaking up the ambiance we've created indoors as well as the glorious panorama outside each window.

What *are* we doing here in Canaan Valley, smack dab in the middle of the West Virginia mountains? Do you really want to know? Then pull up a chair, kick off your shoes, and I'll tell you the story behind *Sweet's Body & SoulCafe and Mountain Store*.

A few years back, while driving through this remote part of the country on my way to a conference in Buckhannon, my soul was hijacked by the sense that somehow my destiny was caught up with this plot of planet Earth, where God did some of creation's finest artwork. So I managed to squeeze together three free hours to shop around for some property. Now it's a sixty-mile drive from Buckhannon—where I was chairing the Northeast Jurisdictional Conference of the United Methodist Church—to Canaan Valley. That left less than one hour to see a couple of parcels and get back to my responsibilities.

While I was driving I wondered, *Why am I doing this?* I didn't have the money to buy a badlyneeded new car, much less land in a little-known, virtually unpopulated region of West Virginia. I didn't even know what I'd do with the property once I had it. I just knew it had to be a part of my life.

Canaan Valley got its name from a nineteenth-century traveler who stumbled into this wilderness Shangri-la. Here he found white oaks growing twenty-four feet in circumference and rutabagas as big as watermelons lounging around on the valley floor. After scouting around the unprecedented lushness of the land and gasping at its breathtaking beauty, he exclaimed in awe and wonderment, "This must surely be the Land of Canaan!" (in Appalachian, that's pronounced *Kah-nane*). Ever since that day, this, the largest high-mountain valley east of the Rockies, has gone by the name of Canaan Valley.

Typical of people who are products of mountain culture, I knew very little of the land beyond the hollow in Greenbrier County where my mother's family-homestead was located. I had never been in Tucker County, the home of Canaan Valley. I'd heard talk that wilderness experts ranked Canaan Valley's beauty and splendor right up there with the celebrity landscapes of Yosemite and Yellowstone, but without ever having experienced Canaan Valley for myself, I didn't believe it. How one drive, one little journey, can change everything.

When I arrived in the valley that cool July afternoon, realtor Bob Andre was waiting for me in his office. We hurried to the two sites he had picked out, and within thirty minutes I had made a selection, signed papers, and was driving back to Buckhannon. To this day, I am Bob's fastest sale.

All the way home I shook my head, wondering what I'd just done and how I'd explain it to Mother, who lived with us at the time. When I got home I told her the whole story, how when I drove through the valley that first time

I felt like a Dalmatian in a firehouse—my juices started flowing, my tail began wagging, and bells rang constantly. Mother sat very calmly, listening to my tale from start to finish without a word. Finally she casually said, "Oh, I know that area quite well. That was one of the areas your grandfather worked when he was a sawyer."

"He did what?" I said in amazement.

You see, my grandfather, George Lemuel Boggs, supported his growing family in the early twentieth century (nine children, seven who lived into adulthood) by working as a sawyer in competition with three of his brothers. It turns out it was my grandfather who carried into the valley some of the saws that eventually cut it down. To this day, Canaan Valley holds the lumbering record for the greatest board-feet-per-square-acre ever to come out of the eastern states. My grandfather and other early loggers and sawyers of West Virginia took one of God's choicest parcels and scalped it bald. From the few pictures I've seen that show the men standing on behemoth trunks with smiles on their faces, one can see how very proud they were of their "accomplishment." So proud, in fact, they boasted that not one twig was left standing when they were done.

That job completed, my grandfather returned to the family homestead, hung up his saws, and started a stay-at-home shift position at the local paper mill. But he left behind in Canaan Valley a landscape completely barren except for an eight-foot-deep humus. The first time lightning struck the valley, the humus caught on fire and burned for thirty years. Through winter snows of two hundred inches and more, the superrich topsoil smoldered right down to the bedrock, where the flames finally flickered out. Then nature took its course and the reseeding and resurrecting began.

Well, as soon as my mother said my grandfather had worked there, I knew why my soul had been held hostage, why my future was hitched to this high mountain valley. I was being summoned to undo some of what my ancestors had innocently done. Even so I wondered, would Revelation's haunting phrase, "The time has come to destroy those who are destroying the earth" (chap. 11) come to pass in my lifetime?

Now understand, no matter how hard we (me and many others, including the U.S. government who, in October 1994, made these 32,000 acres our nation's 500th national wildlife refuge) work to conserve it, Canaan Valley will never be the same as it was before my grandfather and his buddies took down its majestic forest monarchs. That untamed grandeur and magnificence is gone forever. But there is a whole new beauty now, the beauty of resurrection—boreal forests, upland bogs, wetlands 3,200 feet above sea level, clear mountain streams, and tundra-like landforms along the ridges of the mountain tops. The wildlife, too, is diverse, including an ecosystem that is home to migratory birds, wild turkeys, and black bears, as well as the threatened Cheat Mountain salamander, the endangered Virginia northern flying squirrel, and a host of other rare life-forms.

To make a long story short, I borrowed from friends and banks, cashed in my pension fund, and decided to go for broke in bringing Canaan Valley—one of the most beautiful and non-touristy places in America—back to life. It's my legacy to the next generation, and hopefully the next.

So here I sit, smiling at you from the *SoulCafe*. "Cutting edge" for New York City, it's situated in Thomas, West Virginia, an old railroad and mining town (population 200) just outside Canaan Valley. I have no idea what comes next. Life is like a mountain railroad—more detour than route—with lots of backtracks, tangents, missed turns, wrong turns, and even some regrets. Someday, those turns are going to lead many a weary wanderer right up to our front door.

What do we have to offer? you ask.

I'm reminded of something George Orwell wrote in his 1940 journal: "I once played [a rather cruel trick] on a wasp. He was sucking jam on my plate, and I cut him in half. He paid no attention, merely went on with his meal, while a tiny stream of jam trickled out of his severed oesophagus. Only when he tried to fly away did he grasp the dreadful thing that had happened to him. It is the same with modern man. The thing that has been cut away is his soul, and . . . he did not notice it."

Many of us today are stuffing the essence of our beings with the nectars of the world—material things, power, wealth, fame—while at the same time our souls are being snipped off without our even noticing the detachment or interrupting our repast. In the midst of mountainous splendor, the *SoulCafe* is a place of reflection where one can step back and ask how the soul is recovered. After all, God gave us the mountain peaks as one of the soul's native habitats; it is here that perspective is regained and we realize God is near at hand to help us on our journey to spiritual wholeness.

Near, that is, to those who seek.

Come, let us seek together at the *SoulCafe*.

—Leonard Sweet

Chapter 1
IS YOUR CLAY MOIST?

The Potter breathes life into the lump of clay . . .
and the clay says, "make me beautiful,
make me what I am supposed to be. . . ."
And so as the potter I talk to the clay at every step.
The clay becomes a living being, when I put it in my hand.
At birth the clay is without form, and so . . . flexible.
As I build my pot, a child begins to form . . .
and like a child the pot is still pliable
and not yet completely formed.
I add more life-giving clay to my pot, and it grows.
And as with the formative years of youth,
I tug and pull at the clay, to provide the shaping that is so vital.
As with life's path itself, some pots emerge with a struggle . . .
and others with a smooth flow of energy.

—AL QÖYAWAYMA

Why did you buy this book? What are you looking for?

We are a destination-obsessed, goal-possessed culture, and yet we are desperately looking for something. There is a quest for some sort of awakening, a deep hunger for "spiritual" renewal (not everyone defines *spiritual* in the same terms), lurking behind all the scheduled chaos that fills postmodern life. Not all recognize they are searching for something more, but a glance into their activities tells that they are. Others have become so consumed by their spiritual pilgrimage they have dropped out of reality, some for the rest of their lives. Most of us, however, simply press on as time passes by like a speeding train, hoping to find meaning to fill the gnawing emptiness deep inside our souls and becoming perplexingly happy when a spiritual moment erupts at odd moments or in peculiar ways.

Perhaps it is our adherence to a full schedule that has made a boom market of spiritual "quick fixes" in the last few years. Indeed throughout the mid 1990s, spirituality has become a major consumer item. Whenever a spiritual ache twinges or an empty soul growls, we can run to the store and pick up one of two dozen hot sellers on the spiritual-fulfillment shelf. Unfortunately those who really don't know what they're looking for can begin to collect spiritual trinkets like others collect stamps, with nothing of lasting value to show for their purchases.

Take the latest craze over angels, for instance. People collect angel books, angel pillows, angel towels, angel statues, angel jewelry, angel stationery, and angel calendars. But while these things may fill up their homes, the items will never answer the emptiness in their spirits.

Or consider the host of New Agers, who revere the seemingly harmless ancient rituals and religious traditions of planet Earth. Collecting talismans, crystals, pyramids, animal spirit-guides, herbal potions, dream shapers, dream catchers, and shamans along their journey, these folks hope to tap into some spiritual spark that is missing from their technologically processed, time-ticking daily schedules.

Some even look to a star-studded Jesus as the answer to their soul search. Dazzled by the miracles they read about in the Bible, they look to him for health, wealth, and prosperity while ignoring the overwhelming purpose of his life—to be the suffering servant spoken of by the prophet Isaiah, who is even today looking for "a few good disciples."

Today, as in ages past, people look in all kinds of places for fulfillment, or what they think will bring fulfillment. Even the men and women who would become Jesus' followers during his lifetime were attracted to the Master, thinking he would cure their physical and political ills. Yet while Jesus knew there were a lot of wrong reasons as well as wrong ways to go about a spiritual quest, he never shunned anyone or turned anyone away.

Nor does he today.

John, in his letter to the churches concerning God's revelation of Jesus Christ, heard a word from the Lord wherein he describes himself as one knocking (literally "continually knocking") at the door of our hearts. Whoever will take the time to stop and open the door, and invite the living Christ in, will experience eternal communion with God (Rev. 3:20). Jesus doesn't bust the door down. He doesn't shoot it open with an AK-47 assault rifle. He knocks, quietly, continually, and waits for an invitation.

Are you listening for the knock? Are you ready to open the door when it comes? Are you waiting, expectantly, for your hour of visitation?

IS YOUR CLAY MOIST?

When the King James Version of the Bible first appeared in 1611, a London cleric claimed that it "sounds like yesterday's newspaper and denies the divinity and messiahship of Christ." Another chaplain accused the translators of pandering to King James's interest in witchcraft, and when they sailed for the New World in 1620, the Pilgrims refused to carry the King James Version with them.

In 1863, a newspaper editor in Harrisburg, Pennsylvania, traveled thirty-five miles to the wheat fields turned battlefields of Gettysburg, where ten thousand men died in grisly combat, six thousand in the span of three hours. There he heard President Abraham Lincoln proclaim that America was to be a nation whose government was "of the people, by the people, for the people." The next day he wrote in his paper these comments about the Gettysburg Address: "We pass over the silly remarks of the President; for the credit of the nation, we are willing that the veil of oblivion shall be dropped over them and that they should no more be repeated or thought of."

Winston Churchill was not liked by everyone. Welsh liberal Davis Lloyd George snarled that "he would make a drum out of the skin of his mother in order to sound his own praises." But Churchill could stir a crowd as few politicians in his lifetime. After he delivered his "Blood, Sweat and Tears" speech on May 13, 1940, the British diplomat and social critic Harold Nicolson went home and wrote in his diary: "Winston makes a very short statement, but to the point."

IS YOUR CLAY MOIST?

In the thirties of the nineteenth century (1836 to be exact), in the little village of Rushville, New York, a physician named Marcus Whitman heard the call of Christ in the West—a summons to go to those beyond the Mississippi who had never heard the gospel. So he packed his belongings and, with his new wife, set out as a missionary to the Oregon country, where he was destined to become one of the great figures in the history of the Pacific Northwest. That same year, Whitman's pastor wrote this assessment about the activities of his church in his annual report: "Nothing of importance has happened this year. We had one addition to the church, but he married one of our young women, and now they are both gone. So we have one less to report than we did a year ago."

At the very time Orville and Wilbur Wright were flying the first plane in 1903, the astronomer Simon Newcomb confidently concluded an article demonstrating that "no possible combination of known substances, known forms of machinery and known forms of force, can be united in a practical machine by which men shall fly long distances through the air, this seems to the writer as complete as it is possible for the demonstration of any physical fact to be."

IS YOUR CLAY MOIST?

In the thirties of the twentieth century, the two greatest physicists of the modern era and architects of the golden age of theoretical physics, Nobel laureate Paul Dirac and German physicist Werner Heisenberg, traveled around the world. Showing up unannounced at the University of Hawaii during their journey, the president of the university tells the rest of the story a few months later: "A couple of guys turned up, said they were Heisenberg and Dirac, and wanted to give a lecture; but I saw through them and had them shown out."

The Russian-born U.S. violinist Jascha Heifetz (1901–1987), one of the greatest violinists of all time in terms of technical proficiency, once played the violin on a street corner and was hardly noticed. One winter's night, he was scheduled to play in Cleveland when one of those "lake effect" storms off Lake Erie closed roads, making streets impassable. When the concert was about to begin, only one couple sat in the concert hall. The theater manager delayed the curtain for a half hour. Still no more concert goers. Finally, Heifetz stepped in front of the curtain and announced that the concert was called off. The couple protested: "Sir, we have driven over four hours from Dayton for this. Please. Please, won't you *sing* just one number?"

IS YOUR CLAY MOIST?

When a prototype of an invention was demonstrated at the 1939 World's Fair, the *New York Times* reviewer was unimpressed. "The problem with [this invention]," he wrote, "is that the people must sit and keep their eyes glued on a screen; the average American family hasn't time for it." He was reviewing the world premier of television.

An entry in the diary of the world's most famous diarist, Samuel Pepys, reads: "March 1 [1661/62] . . . to the Opera, and there saw . . . for the first time it was ever acted . . . a play of itself the worst that ever I heard in my life, and the worst acted that ever I saw these people do." A little while later, on September 29, 1662, Pepys attended another performance by this same playwright: "The most insipid, ridiculous play that ever I saw in my life," he wrote. The plays he was describing were the premier London performances of William Shakespeare's *Romeo and Juliet* and *A Midsummer Night's Dream.*

IS YOUR CLAY MOIST?

Incidents like these could be multiplied indefinitely. A *New York Times* movie critic called *Lawrence of Arabia*, when it first appeared in 1962, "just a huge lumbering camel opera." August Kekulé's benzene formula was dismissed by several eminent chemists at the time as "a tissue of fancies." Paul Gaugin's Postimpressionist paintings, one of the most decisive steps in the history of twentieth-century art, were scorned by many of his former colleagues. The president of the Linnean Society of London, reporting on their 1858 schedule of meetings (at one of which Charles Darwin and Arthur Wallace had read their papers on natural selection), complained that there had been no striking discoveries that year.

One of the saddest things that can be said of anyone is that greatness passed by, and they did not recognize it. Yet in the words of the literary naturalist and poet Henry David Thoreau:

The morning wind forever

blows;

The poem of creation is

uninterrupted;

But few are the ears that

hear it.

Every human being has at one time or another felt that morning wind blowing by; every one of us has been privy to that uninterrupted poem of creation. Yet how many of our ears have really heard it; how many of our eyes have truly seen it? How many of us consistently snore through all the beauty of the dawning day?

In January 1991 I was invited to attend a joint international meeting between the United Nations and the Club of Rome. Scientists, artists, poets, politicians, and theologians were present to address and redress the twenty-first century. As the heady delegates hobnobbed with and fawned over each other, their conversations locked in Lego-kit-jargon exchanges, one person sat serenely poised in bemused silence, watching the peacock parade of brilliance.

I introduced myself to this solitary figure who radiated such still-in-one-piece energies, but I did not spend much time getting to know him. I hobbled off to schmooze with the "celebrities" and to join their arched conversations, their abstractions about abstractions. Only later did I discover that this person was *the* Al Qöyawayma (pronounced Ko-YAH..wy-mah), one of the greatest potters this continent has ever produced.

The clay of my life was hard.

My subsequent research into this man's art eventually led to my striking upon his philosophy of his life-calling: "The role of my art and life as an artist is to glorify God, our creator. As with our ancestors, Native American artists can help interpret through inner spiritual eyes the world and the environment that surrounds us. Artists will help us to see. They will provide a nonverbal record of history. As a potter I work with the precious earth, the living clay. I too have learned that all things are interconnected."

Al Q's (as his friends call him) many accomplishments, and my pained recognition of a lost moment in my own history, changed my understanding of spiritual leadership forever. While many of my colleagues cannot even remember this man was there, my life has been unalterably transformed by this one visit to the UN in 1991.

> Chance favors the prepared mind.
> —LOUIS PASTEUR

Is your clay moist? Moments of incarnation are as precious as they are passing. How many of us have stood numb and dumb like I did in 1991 while greatness passed by? Could it be our problem is not that the time of greatness has passed, rather that we can't see the greatness that does pass by? How many people have kept on with their lives without missing a step, without changing their pace, without turning their heads or even turning around, while Jesus passed by?

The people of Nazareth watched as one of their own, this artisan/contractor named Jesus, dared to preach, teach, and heal. The large home crowds who heard him teach "were amazed and said, 'Where does he get this from?' and 'What wisdom is this that has been given him?' and 'How does he work such miracles? Is not this the builder, the son of Mary?'" (Mark 6:2–3). It was all "too much for them," as Mark puts it. Or as we might say it today, it was just too far out for them to believe. Thus Jesus' ministry in Galilee came to an inglorious end. "[Jesus] could work no miracle there," and was "taken aback by their want of faith," Mark concludes.

What is the reason for such missed moments? Is it the same reason why Jesus wept over Jerusalem in Luke 19:41–44: we sometimes do not "know the time of [our] visitation"? Is this not something that can be said of every one of us, that Jesus passes by, and we do not recognize him?

How many times does Jesus arrive at our door, and we do not know the hour of our own visitation? Why is it that it can be said of every one of us that we stood in the presence of visitations in various forms and didn't see, didn't believe, or weren't quick to act? We have all been privileged to have had epiphanies pass our way—times when God approached us personally and directly, desiring an encounter that would jump-start our spirits. Why isn't there recognition of the divine when it comes upon us? Why do we have such a hard time seizing the moment, recognizing the glorious appearing for what it is, grasping his garment as he passes, and entering into the joy of the celebration?

Perhaps the best clue to our condition is provided by the story of the ten bridesmaids waiting for the bridegroom to come and escort them to his party, told in Matthew 25:1–13. It was a story Jesus told at Mt. Olivet a few days before his death.

The problem posed by the parable is the same as our problem today: no one knew for sure when the bridegroom would come. He could pick any hour of the day, or any day of the week, and sometimes the waiting stretched over a fortnight. His only obligation was to send a messenger running ahead, shouting to the village, "The bridegroom is coming! The bridegroom is coming!" No amount of planning was adequate to predict when the host would arrive to take everyone to the celebration. That meant the guests had to be prepared. In the parable, the bridegroom was slower in coming than anyone anticipated—he tarried—which meant that the bridal party had to wait as well. When the cry finally came, "The bridegroom is coming!" everyone was sleeping. Hurriedly rising, only five bridesmaids were ready, having extended reserves of oil, etc. The five "foolish" bridesmaids found themselves in the wrong place at the wrong time—trying to purchase extra oil from the store when they should have stored up the extra oil in the first place. When they finally did arrive at the party, they were too late; even now, the finality of Jesus' words continues to clang through the centuries: "And the door was shut" (v. 10 NEB).

Are we letting opportunity after opportunity pass us by? How many times have we been an absentee at "the feast"? Why is it we can't see, much less seize, all the opportunities passing by us? Why do we let greatness pass by? Maybe it's because we want to live planned lives, whereas the Bible teaches us to live prepared lives. To be prepared is to be in the condition and company of the five wise virgins.

 The door that has been closed is not so quickly opened.

—OLD JEWISH PROVERB

Genesis 2 portrays God as the Master Potter, scooping dust out of the earth, adding water, and then breathing that swampland into consciousness. As anyone who saw the movie *Ghost* knows, right after a potter takes a lump of clay and places it on a wheel, the next thing that has to happen if the clay is to be molded is it has to be wetted down. The moisture of the clay is the expression of the clay's receptivity to the potter's will. If the clay remains hard and refuses to allow itself to be moistened, the best potter in the universe cannot fashion a thing of beauty out of it. It will be a crusty clump of clay, unformed and unfashioned forever.

An alternative metaphor is offered to describe this human receptivity to the divine by one of the great mystics in the history of the church, Spanish nun Teresa of Avila, in *The Interior Castle*. She says, "For indeed the soul does no more in this union than does the wax when another impresses a seal on it." Genesis 2 provides for more human-divine interchange than wax and seal, however, which is why the miracle of clay has such profound appeal. For part of the miracle of clay is the fact that the clay itself is an active participant in its own shaping.

But first the clay has to be moist. It must have a yielding nature.

Is the clay of our souls moist? Is our nature yet yielding?

> Reality, in fact, is always something you couldn't have guessed.
> That's one of the reasons I believe Christianity.
> It's a religion you couldn't have guessed.
>
> —C. S. LEWIS

The truth is we don't like being moistened. Moisture is the precursor to molding, and change is uncomfortable for most people. Only God knows the future. That means only God offers refuge against infinite possibilities. But God does not think our thoughts. Therefore our efforts to "think straight" and "plan ahead" are confounded because God denies human attempts at flat, linear predictions of divine unfolding. There is within us and around us something beyond us—something beyond our understanding and beyond our control that has power over our lives and with which we must connect if we are to live whole, abundant lives.

> Whatever you do anyway,
> remember that these things are mysteries
> and that if they were such that we could understand them,
> they wouldn't be worth understanding.
> A God you can understand would be less than yourself.
>
> —FLANNERY O'CONNOR

In a world of change, even change itself is not what it used to be. It is now proceeding exponentially, not incrementally. According to quantum physics, the dynamics of the physical life are spontaneous, not determined; they are not fundamentally matter, but energy; they are not predictable, but a surprise. Werner Heisenberg's Uncertainty Principle is perhaps better named the Mystery Principle since it demonstrates how, at the very core of creation, there is an incomprehensible mystery. Similarly the theory of chaos is a major contribution to the awareness that no physical system, no matter how simple, is beyond behaving in absolutely unpredictable fashion.

How much moreso the mysterious dynamics of the spiritual life. If surprise and departures from the norm are some of the chief characteristics of contemporary physics, then how much more are surprises and departures from the norm to be expected in the spiritual life? Right now God wants to prepare us for something that we cannot possibly understand or predict. Only by accepting "not-knowing" will we be accepted into the heart of existence itself. Only by accepting God's plan, not ours, will we find ultimate fulfillment. In the words of God through the prophet Jeremiah, "I alone know the plans I have for you, plans of peace not of disaster, plans to bring about the future you hope for" (29:11 author's paraphrase).

In the parable of the sower, Jesus taught how the ground must first be prepared before the seed can take root. Yes, the Spirit prepares, but the soil must also yield.

In the parable of the ten bridesmaids, the five "wise" maids were ready for the hour of visitation of the bridegroom because they were prepared for a potentially long wait. God sends to each of us various and sundry windows of opportunity to meet him. All of life's exercises, all the preparations, get us ready to leap forth in faith through these moving, open windows. It is an institutional head-on plunge into the unknown and unpredictable.

Is your clay moist?

> It is not thou that shapest God; it is God
> that shapest thee.
> If then thou are the work of God, await
> the hand of the Artist who does all
> things in due season.
> Offer him thy heart soft and tractable and
> keep the form in which the Artist has
> fashioned thee.
> Let thy clay be moist, lest thou grow hard
> and lose the imprint of his fingers.

Chapter 2
ONIONS AND ARTICHOKES

Always a mask
Held in the slim hand, whitely,
Always she had a mask before her face—
Smiling and sprightly,
The mask.
For years and years I wondered
But dared not ask
And then—
I blundered,
I looked behind the mask,
To find
Nothing—
She had no face.
She had become merely a hand
Holding the mask
With grace.
—HELEN JOSEPH

Onions and artichokes are two of the most interesting vegetables we can handle. Trying to peel an onion is like trying to pet a skunk. It puts up all the resistance it can muster, and often reduces us to such a weepy, stinging state of retreat that the onion becomes unreachable. What do those martyrs who persist in peeling off layer after layer find as the reward for their torture? An onion has no heart, no core, no inner character. It has only layers and layers—masks that resist being ripped off.

Artichokes also have protective coverings, thistle-like petals that must be peeled off. But fully cooked, these layers drop off readily, as if relieved to fall away at the slightest indication that the peeler is truly interested in what lies beneath them. Any taste of the petal leaves no doubt that it is not what one is searching for, although we are encouraged onward by the increasing succulence of the petals the more layers we remove. Those who genuinely seek to get inside the heart of an artichoke are ultimately rewarded with a core that has integrity and character.

Onions and artichokes present a revealing metaphorical glimpse into the true persona of the Christian. While some are layers of love and good works surrounding a heart that is genuinely open, receptive, and packed with God's grace, others are only layer upon layer of pretense with no "heart of flesh" beneath.

God spoke some very provocative words to Israel through the prophet Ezekiel regarding renewal. He said in order for renewal to take place, their hearts would have to be transformed from a "heart of stone" to a "heart of flesh" (Ezekiel 36:26–27). A heart of stone is callous to sin and compassion. A heart of flesh is sensitive to God's own heart, and open to the prompting to the Holy Spirit. A little further in the scriptural text (chap. 37), this idea of transformation is further illustrated in the vision of the dry bones that are brought back to life through the renewal of the Holy Spirit.

We are, at times, dry bones. We are hearts of stone. In order for renewal and relationship to begin, we need our hearts transformed. But how?

We live in a "choice-driven" society. Did you know, for instance, there are nearly twenty different kinds of Kleenex, forty different varieties of Tylenol, and over 700 different makes and models of cars in the U.S. alone?

More then ever before, an increasing percentage of our time is spent simply choosing between various options in any given decision.

I like having choices, but am uneasy over the way people are creating for themselves a "choice morality," pulling down values like we pull items down from the supermarket shelves. I am anxious about the way people are falling head-over-heels in love with do-it-yourself deities, which they have crafted in their own image. In the same way, I am concerned about the way many Christians pinball around from church to church, looking for the one that will ring their bells and toot their whistles, and then leaving it the first time it yanks their chains.

As important as choice is, it must not become a belief system, a religion in and of itself. The last time I read my Bible, it did not say, "And now there abides faith, hope, love and choice, but the greatest of these is choice." The purpose of life is not to make choices; the purpose of life is to glorify God and enjoy God forever. But that is accomplished *through* our choices.

> There comes a midnight hour when all must unmask.
> —SØREN KIERKEGAARD

Lee Atwater (1951–1991), known as a brutal, consummate political strategist and hardball Republican National Committee chair, became a repentant believer and foe of "DC-mentality" before he died of brain cancer. Before he died, he said, "I acquired more [wealth, power, and prestige] than most. But you can acquire all you want, and still feel empty. It took a deadly illness to put me eye to eye with that truth, but it is a truth that the country, caught up in its ruthless ambitions and moral decay, can learn on my dime. [The leaders of the '90s must] speak to the spiritual vacuum at the heart of American society. . . . What is missing in society is what was missing in me: a little heart."

What Atwater discovered is true: what we choose to allow into our thoughts and beings literally changes us from the inside out. When he chose to allow Christ access to his heart as Lord, his eyes were opened to the ruthless "hunger" that had, to that point, ruled his life. His life changed because his heart was transformed.

Even kids understand this concept, thanks to Disney's film depiction of Aladdin's magical genie. In the movie, a thought to the genie (Robin Williams) instantly transformed his being, even his shape. Think Groucho Marx, and the genie became Groucho Marx. Think of Arsenio Hall and the genie became Arsenio. Think of hell, and the genie became a fiery inferno.

In 1993, this concept was quite graphically illustrated in the celebrated trial of two boys, age ten, who murdered a toddler in Liverpool, England. On February 12, 1993, James Bulger, one month shy of his third birthday, was strolling in his gray trainer pants in a shopping mall in Bootle. During the trial, the entire world watched in horror as the mall's security video captured the images of two boys—Jon Venables and Bobby Thompson—as they grabbed James's hand and lead him out of the mall. They walked him two or three miles across Liverpool to a railroad track, where they beat him to death with stones, bricks, and a twenty-two pound fishplate, then strapped him to the rails for an oncoming train to run over. The boys were found guilty; the imprint of one of Bobby's shoes was clearly defined on James's cheek.

Why did these two ten-year-olds do what they did? The judge at the trial, Sir Michael Morland, believes he knew. It seems that Jon Venables' father had just rented *Child's Play 3*, a slice-and-dice horror movie featuring a demonic doll named "Chucky" come to life. In the judge's words, "It is not for me to pass judgement on their upbringing, but I suspect that exposure to violent video films may in part be an explanation."

Like the saying goes, "garbage in—garbage out." But there's another side to that coin—more powerful than the garbage law—found in 2 Corinthians 5:17. "Therefore, if anyone is in Christ, he is a new creation; old things have passed away, behold, all things have become new." This is salvation. This is transformation. This is a one-time act; this is an on-going process. Choose to give Christ access to your heart, and stone becomes flesh. Old thoughts, attitudes, and concerns metamorphosize into new ones.

[God] gave them what they asked, but sent a wasting disease among them.

—PSALM 106:15

There are at least two areas of life that many American Christians are obsessed with to the detriment of their souls: success and security, especially financial security.

SUCCESS

Do you remember when you were little? When you were too small and young to do certain jobs or chores around the house? How exotic, exciting, and enticing those tasks appeared! If only you were big enough to run the vacuum cleaner or push the lawn mower, or reach the really high windows with a ten-foot ladder. Two-year-olds love to get pint-sized mops and brooms and act out all the work that goes along with cleaning the house. How the allure fades fast!

As we grow older and work harder and harder to attain our goals, it slowly begins to dawn on us that as we give more of our lives to working our way up the ladder of success, the less satisfied we are with the prize once we've got it! Instead of enjoying it, we realize it has become just another new responsibility, another step up the ladder. "Success" has still alluded us and is somewhere else; or as an old French proverb puts it, "You not only have to want what you want, you have to want what you want leads to."

Unfortunately, we've also been willing to strap our Christianity—our missions, our ministries, our churches, our souls—satisfied with the results. The congregation is never big enough and they never give enough. There are not enough "volunteers."

What makes for spiritual success? According to the secular success model, it must mean reaching huge numbers of people; being able to broadcast the gospel as far and fast as possible; developing church programming that thrives and grows; finding a harmonious, beautiful, forward-looking, upward-thinking church home for worship. Surely these are the markers of a successful ministry or mission. But if these truly are the signs of Christian success, then Jesus must necessarily be counted as a colossal failure:

- Instead of establishing a "Center for Religious Teachings," which could pull students and wisdom-seekers from all over to a central location, Jesus chose to wander the countryside, hardly spending the night in the same place twice. The crowds were always trying to keep up with him.

- Instead of organizing a hierarchy for training scores and scores of followers, Jesus chose only twelve disciples and provided them with strange, "on-the-road" instruction.

- Instead of playing up his miraculous strength and superior wisdom, the wonder and power of his true identity, Jesus chose to appear before the world almost anonymously, as a simple, dusty craftsman, rabbi-of-sorts, and out-of-sorts leader.

Jesus failed to capitalize on a scenario ripe for success. In fact, when this fact was pointed out to him, he rejected the world's view of success completely. Why? Because successes are those things that can be calculated, calibrated, and counted up. Successful ministry in Jesus' eyes did not equate to a number, but to human hearts that were changed, one by one. He was the ultimate servant, and service should never be quantified. The point of service is to offer yourself without counting the cost or tallying the results.

In the parable of the mustard seed (Matt. 13:31–32), Jesus speaks only about our responsibility to sow the seed of faith, to be out there spreading the good news. It is God's responsibility to reap. We are called to plant the seed, but we cannot guarantee the harvest. As mere humans we cannot possibly know the results of our sowing until the eternal harvest, which is brought about by God alone. We will be judged, not by the results of that harvest, but on the sincerity of our sowing. If this is true, then there is no success or failure in God's kingdom; those are the devil's inventions. Jesus never worried about struggling up or slipping down any ladder, he was only concerned with lowering himself toward those in need and extending himself forward into God's service.

If indeed success is a ladder, then service is a chute and a carpet—a chute of free-falling grace and a "magic" carpet because it continues to unfurl and unfold without end as the chute winds its way through humanity. Commitment to a life of service means parachuting into the war zones of the world and extending the welcome mat of God's love and sacrifice to the door of every home and every heart. This is the mission Jesus offers us: downwardly mobile, forward-reaching service, not upward-struggling success.

One of my perks was a company car and driver,
and I was inordinately proud of this badge of success.
I loved to give my associates rides—what's a perk without some strutting?
And I wanted my driver to be another friendly admirer,
part of my supportive audience.
No matter how much I tried to chat him up,
however, he remained distant, responding correctly but coolly.
Finally, I asked him if there was a problem.
Had I offended him in some way?
He tried to duck the question but eventually responded
with classic New York directness. He said,
"All you seem to think about or do is work,
and it doesn't even look like you enjoy yourself.
I guess you're nice enough, but frankly, from my point of view,
your life is real boring."

—JOHN R. O'NEIL

SECURITY

There has been a lot of tongue wagging going on lately about "The Spoiling of America." This is not a concern about water pollution or unchecked deforestation; it is about children—our swelling population of *spoiled* children. Consider the following:

- How big a collection of Power-Rangers does your five-year-old need?

- How many Barbie dolls does it take to satisfy a nine-year-old?

- How much money must really be spent on entertainment at your eleven-year-old's birthday party?

- How many sports and hobbies must you fully outfit your four-teen-year-old for?

- How important is it that a new car be in the driveway on the day your sixteen-year-old gets a driver's license?

- How much longer can you expect to be financially responsible for your college-bound eighteen-year-old, or your graduate-school-bound twenty-two-year-old?

Think this is just about children? Think hard and guess again. What spoiled children and the spoiled adults they become find out is that "more" adds up to less and less. Less satisfaction, less joy, less enthusiasm, less happiness. People who have based their lives on "bottom-line living"—where the only thing that really counts is that bottom-line tally ("The one with the most toys at the end, wins," as one bumper sticker put it)—eventually "bottom-out" on the realization that more is not necessarily better. Gradually their devotion to a "god of more" just doesn't seem like enough.

Christian psychologist David G. Meyers, in his book *The Pursuit of Happiness: Who is Happy—and Why*, studied this issue and made these remarks in his consumer report on happiness: The things that enable you to be happy are not how much money you make, or how many possessions you own, or whether you are highly educated, or whether you are old or young. Meyers summed up his report by saying that while per capita income in America more than doubled in real terms between 1957 and 1990, the number of Americans who reported being "very happy" remained the same—at one-third. In other words, having more did not answer our deepest yearnings or fulfill our deepest needs.

The American Dream, defined in terms of material things, has become The American Nightmare. The best of times materially they may be, but they seem more like the worst of times spiritually. In Meyers' words:

- Never has a culture experienced such comfort and opportunity, or such massive genocide and environmental devastation.

- Never has a technology given us so many conveniences, or such terrible instruments of degradation and destruction.

- Never have we been so self-reliant, or so lonely.

- Never have we seemed so free, or our prisons so overstuffed.

- Never have we had so much education, or such high rates of teen delinquency, despair and suicide.

- Never have we been so sophisticated about pleasure, or so likely to suffer broken or miserable marriages.

Meyers concluded his study of happiness with these words: "Well-being is found in the renewal of disciplined lifestyles, committed relationships and the receiving and giving of acceptance. To experience deep well-being is to be self-confident yet unself-conscious, self-giving yet self-respecting, realistic yet hope-filled."

This concept is borne out in the story of the rich young man who had everything materially anyone could wish for, even led a "good" life, but was dismayed when Jesus told him that to achieve eternal life, he must give everything away and follow Jesus. The dominant moral of the story is riches can't buy a person's way into heaven. But a subtle subtext is that Jesus knew the man's riches could not ultimately satisfy the craving in his soul, the gnawing at his spirit, which are what drew the man to Jesus in the first place. For this rich young man, only the giving up of his "security blanket" of wealth would quench the fire of discontent in his innermost being.

Are you among those who have "bottomed-out" on "bottom-living?" Are you ready to try finding a solid-rock foundation instead of banking on some bank account? Or are you still hoping that fulfillment, love, inspiration, and commitment can be purchased for a price?

My generation strikes me as self-absorbed. You hear them at the grocery store deliberating the balsamic vinegar and the olive oils . . . and you think, "These people probably subscribe to an olive oil magazine called New Dimension." They are people with too much money and very little character, people who are all sensibility and no sense, all nostalgia and no history, the people my Aunt Eleanor used to call "a $10 haircut on a 59-cent head"—people I would call yuppie swine.

—Garrison Keillor, Vanity Fair, July 1994.

There is plenty of evidence pointing to the predominance of the "bottom-line," "more-is-good" mentality in our culture. More and more of us are buying into the new version of the American Dream—the one that just costs a dollar every evening—the lottery. A watershed in American history has been reached: The number one peak experience now sought by Americans is not falling in love, it's winning the lottery. Since the beginning of the lottery, three out of four Americans have bought lottery tickets. In 1994 alone, one hundred million Americans in thirty-six states and the District of Columbia spent $30 billion in tickets. Yet only 173 millionaires have been produced in twelve years from lottery winnings.

A game-theory professor once calculated the odds of winning are the same as a poker player's chance of drawing four royal flushes in a row, all in spades—then getting up from the card table and meeting four strangers, all with the same birthday. Despite the lousy odds and its addictive potential, the myth of a big win bringing everything ever dreamed of still persists. So do big winners get a dream-come-true? An Illinois study developed a method of determining "general happiness" and studied those who won lotteries, those who were victims of accidents, and those who had nothing extreme happen to them. The least happy? The lottery winners.

The Roper polling company regularly polls Americans on how much money they think they will need to fulfill their dreams. In 1995, the median sum mentioned was $102,000 a year. But the number responding $1 million or more a year had doubled since the previous year.

Regarding both success and security for the Christian disciple the biblical message is clear—"count the cost of discipleship," then throw away the calculator. Just as Mary Magdalene poured out her expensive ointment without counting the cost, so we are to pour our precious love on the vulnerable and invaluable—we are to be spendthrifts with love; reckless with forgiveness; imprudent with passion.

How do we decide where to pour out our love? How do we determine what is our mission together? How do we look for our mission, our future, as individuals and as a church? Joanna Macy, an educator, ecologist, and author, suggests three directions:

1. Work with your passion. What do you care about? What makes your heart sing? What gets you outside yourself? Throw yourself into your passion—without counting the cost.

2. Work with your pain. Where have you been, so that you know where others have been? Where have you been broken? Claim your pain—without counting the cost.

3. Work with what is at hand. What has God given you that is all around you? There is no perfect "job-charm." Find purpose in the small things—without counting the cost.

> Within my earthly temple, there's a crowd;
> There's one of us that's humble, one that's proud;
> There's one that's broken-hearted for his sins;
> There's one that, unrepentant, sits and grins;
> There's one that loves his neighbor as himself
> And one that cares for naught but fame and self.
> From much corroding care I should be free
> If I could once determine which is me.
>
> —EDWARD SANFORD MARTIN

Chapter 3
DISCIPLESHIP = RELATIONSHIP

The family in America is in crisis. The American family is at risk. Over the last half decade in this country, "family values" has become the hot button in both the educational and political arenas. The lack of it is being blamed for everything from the rise in violent crimes perpetrated by young kids and teens to the demise of the democratic society in this country.

Are you tired of hearing that? Before you close your ears (and turn the page), let me suggest one more, perhaps different, thought.

In typical postmodern fashion, where opposite things happen at the same time without being contradictory, Christians today need to build stronger family life while at the same time not make family into a new idolatry. Certainly the church needs to "focus on the family" (as one organization puts it), but at the same time it must resist the temptation to fixate on the family to the exclusion of God. The fact is, despite the realities of a soaring divorce rate, broken families, abused children, and neglected "together time," our culture is beginning to make the family into one of the most revered idols at which we kneel and worship.

In "Confronting the Idolatry of the Family," theologian Janet Fishburn declares that we have succeeded in elevating an idealized version of the family over and above God. Yet the Bible is clear: Nothing must come between God and us or before our faith in God. So as we build a stronger focus on the family, let us not give family first place in our lives.

In his must-read book *Sacred Cows Make Gourmet Burgers,* Bill Easum writes, "Family is never a priority issue in the Scriptures. It is mentioned only six times in the New Testament and never in relation to a congregation. Family is always secondary to Christ's claim on us. On several occasions, Jesus deemphasized the importance of family, saying that family obligations came behind the demands of discipleship."

In fact, Jesus put the disciples' obligations to the mission of the kingdom before caring for dead family members (Matt. 8:22); he said anyone wishing to be his disciple must be willing to "hate" his father, mother, wife, and siblings (Luke 14:26); he even said he came to cause divisions in the family (Matt. 10:35). The most emphatic definition of family, according to Jesus, is explained in Matthew 12:46–50, when he stated that "Whoever does the will of my Father in heaven is my brother, and sister, and mother."

How can these two ideologies—pro-family and pro-kingdom mission—harmonize, then, if they're so diametrically opposed? Rather than pulling inward to build up our families—which is what much of the pro-family propagandists are bidding us to do—I believe the answer lies in spreading outward to incorporate the entire community of relationships into our families.

I was sitting on a beach one summer day, watching two children, a boy and a girl, playing in the sand. They were hard at work, by the water's edge, building an elaborate sand castle with gates and towers and moats and internal passages.
Just when they had nearly finished their project, a big wave came along and knocked it down, reducing it to a heap of wet sand. I expected the children to burst into tears, devastated by what had happened to all their hard work.

But they surprised me. Instead, they ran up the shore away from the water, laughing and holding hands, and sat down to build another castle.

I realized that they had taught me an important lesson. All the things in our lives, all the complicated structures we spend so much time and energy creating, are built on sand. Only our relationships to other people endure. Sooner or later, the wave will come along and knock down what we have worked so hard to build up. When that happens, only the person who has somebody's hand to hold will be able to laugh.

—Rabbi Harold S. Kushner

Few stories tell the biblical interpretation of "relationship" better than the above, with its simple moral of holding hands. Whether these two children are siblings or merely friends, the message is clear: holding hands makes the world easier to handle. Holding hands eases hurt, pain, and disappointment. Holding hands helps deter wrong actions. Holding hands allows the frightened to move more readily toward security in God.

Throughout the Gospels, Jesus not only met people where they were physically, going out into the cities, villages, and surrounding countryside for his audience, he met them where they were emotionally, as well. He let the weeping woman anoint his feet with ointment and tears; he healed the crowds and soothed their troubled spirits before delivering a sermon; he provided them with physical nourishment; he raised their dead out of compassion. Jesus constantly and consistently picked up others out of the mire of sorrow, sin, illness, and despair. He never stood on ceremony, rather he journeyed alongside people wherever their paths took them. In short, he loved them.

 To love another person is to help him to love God.

—Søren Kierkegaard

When the Bible defines God as "love" and us as created in God's image, it is tipping us off to something extremely important. Love means relationship. God made us to be in relationship. When Jesus called men and women to be his disciples, he called them to the same task, to be in relationship with the world around them. To be a disciple of Jesus Christ means to live life not standing against, or closing in, or shutting out, but walking alongside. The life of a disciple is a double movement—a life of dying with Christ and a life of rising with Christ; a life of travail and a life of enjoyment; a life of emptying oneself and a life of utter fulfillment; a life of taking up one's cross and crying, and a life of taking up one's bed and rejoicing.

There are three types of relationships we must work to develop in our lives, each with its own important role in keeping not only ourselves healthy, but our families and community healthy, as well. These three types of relationships point us in three different directions:

Outward: These are our purely social encounters, our daily experiences of living in the world with others.

Inward: This is how we relate to our inner self, the person we are when no one is looking.

Upward: Our relationship with God, how we meet and experience the divine in our everyday life.

> Our duty is not to see through one another,
> but to see one another through.

A relationship is established when a genuine connection is made. You can have personal relationships with each person you encounter in your life, no matter how long or brief the contact. Whether it's the bank teller, mail carrier, dry cleaner, or checkout clerk at the grocery store, relationship can be meaningful. How? By living deliberately. Look people in the eye as you talk to them (then ask yourself what was their eye color); if they have a name tag on, look at it, then call them by name in the course of conversation; develop a more meaningful response to end conversation than the superficial "Have a good day" we frequently hear; make sure your "How are you?" is sincere and heartfelt, and listen for the response.

I believe there are three sources of distraction that can keep us from having genuine, personal relationships with others. They are hurry, worry, and slurry.

HURRY

In our go-twenty-different-directions-at-once society, hurry can thwart the best intentions at relationship. It destroys our outward, social connections by causing us to commit one of the greatest possible sins against our neighbors—ignoring them. We grab our packages from the grocery clerk and run. We pack so many errands into our lunch hour that we're already halfway out the door before any of our transactions are even completed. When we arrive home after a hectic day, we scurry to catch a snippet of news, get food on the table, or get one more chore in the garage done before heading out the door again to another appointment.

In order to create a life full of deep and rich personal relationships, we must take every human encounter seriously. Making a bank deposit isn't just a financial transaction, it is a personal encounter of trust.

In the words of former Speaker of the House Sam Rayburn, the three most important words in the English language may very well be, "Wait a minute."

WORRY

Of the three distractions, worry is perhaps the most insidious. It destroys our capability for making meaningful relationships with others from the inside out. Worry spirals our attention inward, focusing our energies only on ourselves and our own concerns.

It is next to impossible to genuinely connect with another human being when our minds are a thousand miles away. Being "present" for another is a minimum daily requirement for establishing relationships outside ourselves.

SLURRY

The third distraction, slurry, muddies perspective. It is the stuff that clogs up our lives and clouds our vision, making it impossible for us to see further than the tiny world of our own concerns, needs, and desires. The muck and madness that normally infiltrate daily life can keep us from raising up our eyes and experiencing the presence of the divine, from the most mundane of interactions to the most crucial.

Besides interfering with our direct relationships, slurry can interfere with, or castrate altogether, our indirect relationships as well. For instance, it's difficult to care about hunger and homelessness in another part of the world (or even in our own neighborhood) when we are single-mindedly attending to the task of getting our children to the next soccer game or ourselves to that second or third job so we can maintain a relatively luxurious standard of living.

Tweak these three distractions just a bit, and they are just as appropriate to our inward and upward relationships.

All of us have met someone at one time or another who we would describe as "out of touch with himself" or "out of touch with her feelings," people who never take the time to ask themselves how they feel physically or emotionally, or what their own opinion is about a particular subject. Hurry keeps us from the age-old pastime called "journaling," where we evaluate ourselves in the privacy of our own closet. Hurry also causes us to run from crisis to crisis putting out fires rather than doing the expedient thing which is talking to the "Man upstairs," the one who is ultimately in control of everything.

Worry and slurry distort reality, in different ways, so that our direction becomes unfocused; our thinking, blurred. In this state, it's hard to know when we're in touch with ourselves or God, and it's impossible to be in a posture of listening for God's guidance and direction.

Granted, the idea of slowing down and refocusing on these three aspects of relationship may not be a pleasant thought. Everything we must do to fulfill all our daily obligations is overwhelming, and to ask that the train move slower is like saying to lie down and let it run us over! Not exactly. But it does mean that somewhere along the way, some sacrifices will have to be made. Be of good cheer—God made the greatest sacrifice of all and knows what you're going through. Self-sacrifice is critical to leading an enriched, Spirit-filled life.

Someone once asked Albert Schweitzer to name the greatest person alive in the world at that moment. The good doctor, whom many would have named as deserving the honor, replied quietly: "The greatest person alive in the world at this moment is some unknown individual in some obscure place who, at this hour, has gone in love to be with another person in need."

Jesus was called by God and destined for a unique sacrificial role. But consummating this plan did not mean embracing a doormat mentality. On John Denver's early album, *Poems, Prayers and Promises,* the song "Gospel Changes" contains the line: "Jesus did not doubt his gifts." Jesus expressed himself; he fulfilled himself. Jesus could act as a powerful, compelling leader while calling all who would listen to servanthood because he was first a servant of God. It was on the strength of that relationship with the divine that Jesus was able to make himself the "suffering servant" for all humanity.

Just as Jesus fully developed his gifts, his genius, through self-sacrifice, Christians are called to embody that same sacrificial attitude. Faithfulness to Christ's mission and message does not mandate a lifetime spent under the heel of abusive people and powers, where the notion of genuine servanthood is passive acceptance of any and all exploitation. If we would seek to imitate Christ, to follow in his footsteps, we must first strive to develop our own unique gifts and our own special "genius" to their maximum potentials. If we wish to become suffering servants along with Jesus, we must first seek to be the kind of servant to God that Jesus was, and that he intends us to be.

Unfortunately there are a lot of people so wrapped up in discovering who they are that they forget where they're going and where they stand, in relationship and in community. The great genius of Jesus was that he became more fully himself as he offered more and more of himself to others. This is the Christian paradox of self-expression and self-sacrifice that Jesus embodied—we become more genuinely the person God intended as we extend ourselves in sacrificial love and service to others.

This means striking the right balance between the two, which isn't easy. In music, the concept of "two choirs" was established long ago. Composers and directors learned that a deeper complexity and meaning could be drawn from two different pieces of music performed simultaneously than could ever be achieved by two single performances. The power of two choirs, singing distinctly different yet complementary pieces at one another, does more than simply offer two melodies at once. It transforms each piece and creates an entirely new composition with a life and power all its own.

There should be "two choirs" at work in the soul of Christians as well. On one side they should hear the sweet sound of a call to full self-expression and personal development. In Christ, Christians are free to discover the full extent of their selves and their gifts. On the other side, they should hear another choir calling them to practice self-sacrifice. The defining character of a Christian is as a servant, not as a master—and it is only in service to others that the Christian becomes most fully Christlike.

> Accustom yourself continually to make many acts of love,
> for they enkindle and melt the soul.
>
> —TERESA OF AVILA

Sacrifice comes into play when the Holy Spirit prods us to make choices about how we will live each day in our quest for being in harmony with God's mandate to live in concert with Christ's nature. Inevitably these choices will affect our relationships. When it comes to expressing the idea of an open attitude toward giving of oneself for the benefit of relationship with others, I can think of no better example than the traditional "empty chair."

In the Jewish tradition, the empty chair is a permanent fixture in the greatest thanksgiving feast of the year—the Passover seder. During the meal, an empty chair is set at the seder table and the front door left slightly ajar, symbolically welcoming Elijah to join in the feast.

In the Christian tradition, every Sabbath, or Sunday, is a thanksgiving feast, or should be. Unfortunately, in this hustle-bustle, postmodern society, the festive atmosphere of the once-traditional Sunday celebration has been lost. But in bygone days, Sunday was to be passed in worship, fellowship, and "Sunday dinner," where friends and relatives gathered to share a meal in grateful thanksgiving to God. In Sabbath-observant, church-going families, Sunday was the one day the family planned to spend together, first at church, then at home with the "extended family" or close friends. With a full house and expectant stomachs, Sunday dinner was a meal guaranteed to offer the magic combination of old favorites and once-a-week specialties. Every family had its own traditions: fried chicken, pot roast, pasta.

But for many families, mine included, another tradition played out Sunday after Sunday, similar to the Jewish Passover seder. An empty chair stood at the table, ready to be filled or simply to be gazed at as a reminder that no matter how many people were already present, there was always room and food enough for one more. Even if there wasn't physically an empty chair (some days we had so many people, we used them all up!), there was an extra plate and extra portions of food in case a visitor showed up. Sometimes unexpected relatives or friends did come, but the idea was that even if it were a mere acquaintance or total stranger, he would be welcome.

Sadly, one of the greatest growth indicators in America seems to be the burgeoning of its underclasses—those with the severest cases of the "have nots." True, there are those growing richer than rich, stockpiling millions the way the rest of us stockpile cans for recycling. But there are far more who are so desperately poor, so utterly destitute, that even the barest essentials for existence are beyond their grasp. The only thing equitable about this division is that it seems to cross all ethnic and racial lines. In both black and white America, a small but growing percentage of the population is amassing fortunes while a small but ever-growing number is amassing misery.

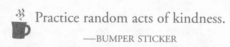 Practice random acts of kindness.
—BUMPER STICKER

In her popular 1971 book *Hidden Art,* Edith Schaeffer, wife of the famous theologian Francis Schaeffer, spoke of the art of hospitality, making ourselves available to whomever God directs our way. Be they family, neighbors, or the homeless man in the park, she urged her readers to share their own "hidden art" talents of infusing an open heart and attitude into life in order to share Christ with others.

Where are our empty chairs? Where are our extra portions?

Why is it we can find room for one more holiday party, one more piece of turkey, one more car in the driveway, one more charge on the credit card . . . while shutting our hearts and finding there is no more time to give, no more bounty to share, no more fellowship to extend?

What will it take to get us to make room for one more name on our "visit" list, one more personal note jotted on a Christmas card, one more hour of volunteer work to better someone else's life, one more person in our hearts?

Room at the table, room in our hearts.

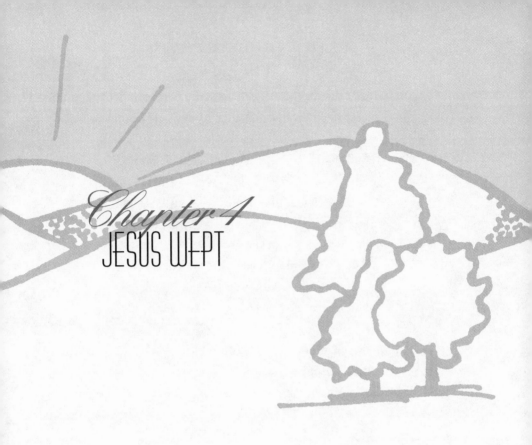

Chapter 4
JESUS WEPT

What is it that makes you cry out in anguish or rage? Watching the film industry, it's obvious that crying is in vogue these days, even for men. But are we getting worked up over the right things?

Jesus wept over the Jews' lack of recognition of the incarnate God among them, to save them from their sins and to renew a right relationship between themselves and God. The Triumphal Entry ended in tears because Jesus' own people could not recognize the Way, the Truth, and the Life when it stared them in the face. He became infuriated with the sellers of sacrificial animals and the money changers in the temple, who made a mockery of God-ordained temple rituals. He cried with compassion over the death of his friend Lazarus, and he wept on the cross.

But Jesus reserved his fiercest emotions for those people who took advantage of the "little ones," be they literally small children or the helpless in society or "babies" in the faith, causing them to stumble. Hear his warning:

And whoever causes one of these little ones who believe in Me to stumble,
it would be better for him if a millstone were hung around his neck,
and he were thrown into the sea.
And if your hand makes you sin, cut it off.
It is better for you to enter into [eternal] life maimed,
than having two hands, to go to hell,
into the fire that shall never be quenched—
where "their worm does not die and the fire is not quenched."
And if your foot makes you sin, cut it off.
It is better for you to enter into [eternal] life lame,
than having two feet, to be cast into hell,
into the fire that shall never be quenched—
where "their worm does not die and the fire is not quenched."
And if your eye makes you sin, pluck it out.
It is better for you to enter the kingdom of God with one eye,
than having two eyes, to be cast into hell fire—where "their worm does not
die and the fire is not quenched."
For everyone will be seasoned with fire, and every sacrifice will be seasoned
with salt. Salt is good, but if the salt loses its flavor, how will you season it?
Have salt in yourselves, and have peace with one another.

—MARK 9:42–50 NKJV

Many people quote the second half of this passage—relating to the abhorrence of sin and the extent to which we should avoid it—without connecting it to the first portion about causing others to stumble, but Jesus made no such distinction. They belong together. In theatrical terms, Jesus' words seem melodramatic or operatic. Spoken with such depth of feeling and emotion, they cannot be read and applied without equal force. *Time* magazine defines *opera* as being "performed at peak volume because the feelings it surveys are big and deep. Matters of lust and death are too important to be spoken; they must be sung, shouted, thundered, wept—and shown, in all their delicious force."

Indeed, sometimes Jesus used exaggerated notions and actions to make his disciples face the gravity of a situation. The Jesus of mercy and forgiveness was suddenly using images of force and fury to illustrate how deep his emotions ran on the subject of sin and misguiding others. Those who willfully erect stumbling blocks, whose actions hinder the progress of "little ones," are declared better off at the bottom of the sea with a stone about their necks. So intense were Jesus' emotions for this circle of society, in fact, that he went on to advise the ancient mechanism of *pars pro toto* (partial sacrifice for the sake of survival in a situation of pursuit, of threat and anxiety) to behavior that would lead others astray.

In the ancient world, *pars pro toto* (especially finger-sacrifice) was not unknown. Antiquity's most celebrated hypochondriac, Aelius Aristides, was instructed in a dream that to save his life he should "cut a piece of his body for the sake of the whole," but that he could dedicate his ring finger instead. But Jesus was the first to talk about *pars pro toto* in the context of sparing others from harm rather than oneself. In unprecedented fashion, Jesus recommended the pain and humiliation of permanent maiming as a positive alternative, not for the sake of self-survival, but for the protection and preservation of the little ones.

In that time, this was a drastic course of action. That Jesus' greatest anger, his darkest emotions, his bitterest tears were reserved for those who took advantage of the little ones illustrated God's deep-seated love for these members of society. Jesus did not try to curb his tongue when castigating those who took unfair advantage of or practiced outright abuse against these little ones of the world. Neither was he ashamed to let the fierceness of his feelings turn to tears of compassion and love for all the little ones who stumble and struggle in this world.

When I was growing up, males learned that "real men don't cry." Admonitions like "Get control of yourself" and "Stop crying" helped wean the weeping out of us. Then we found out that because "real men don't cry," men died earlier than women. A life-flood of tears, it turned out, is the life-blood of health, joy, and strength. So today men are no longer embarrassed about crying big fat tears. Secular songwriter/singer Babyface boasts that "I try to cry when I write." But over what? Spilt beer! It's sappy sentimentality or self-directed, feel-sorry-for-me scenarios that work the secular world up into tears.

What makes us cry, Church? Is our crying really nothing more than wanting what the world has, wanting what we used to have—the prestige, the preeminence, the power and the perks that came with a Christendom church? Or is our crying based on the kinds of attitudes and activities that brought the sting of tongue to Jesus' mouth, the sting of tears to his eyes? Three of the four Gospels read, "Jesus wept," words that have been a mystery down through the ages.

One of my favorite writers, Monica Furlong, wrote a book of her memories of growing up Christian, which she entitled *Our Childhood's Pattern*. The book is based on the fourth verse of Mrs. Alexander's nativity hymn for children, "Once in Royal David's City," the verse most often cut:

> For he is our childhood's pattern:
> Day by day like us he grew;
> He was little, weak and helpless,
> Tears and smiles like us he knew;
> And he feeleth for our sadness,
> And he shareth in our gladness.

An emotional Jesus—breaking into a smile, bursting into tears of sorrow and chagrin—is the Savior we serve; not the "no crying he makes" Savior portrayed in another popular carol. The image of an emotional Jesus confessed by the early church contrasted dramatically with the prevailing Roman ideals of tearlessness and stoicism. Romans like Dictys the Cretan even rewrote the story of Philoctetes so that he never flinched in the face of suffering. They used Jesus' "cry baby" behavior on the cross as evidence that he could not be divine, and they used the volatile images of Jesus' disciples like Peter who "wept bitterly" over his denial of his master as proof that Christians were weak and not to be trusted.

So what really makes us cry, Church? What makes us sad? What makes us glad? What makes us mad? These little ones may seem insignificant in the scheme of secular success, but in the Lord's eyes they are of momentous importance.

But how does one begin to change a thought, an attitude, an action? How does one *begin* to care?

Tears are a biological gift of God.
They are a physical means for expressing emotional
and spiritual experience. But it is hard to know what to do with them.
If we indulge our tears, we cultivate self-pity.
If we suppress our tears, we lose touch with our feelings.
But if we pray our tears, we enter into sadness that integrates our sorrows
with our Lord's sorrows and discover both the source of
and the relief from our sadness.
—EUGENE H. PETERSON

Frederick Buechner tells the story of William Booth's sleepless night that changed his life forever. Booth lay suffering from a severe case of insomnia one night in his comfortable London home when he decided to go out for a walk. He journeyed into a part of London he had never walked through— the poor section. He spent the rest of the night seeing sights and smelling odors he had never before experienced.

When he arrived home in the early hours of the morning, his wife Katherine was almost frantic. "Where in the world have you been?" she cried out.

He replied, "Katherine, I've been to hell, I've been to hell!" He then told her what he'd seen, and together they founded the Salvation Army.

Whenever you find tears in your eyes, especially unexpected tears,
it is well to pay the closest attention.
They are not only telling you something about the secret of who you are,
but more often than not, God is speaking to you through them
of the mystery of where you have come from
and is summoning you to where, if your soul is to be saved,
you should go next.

Have you been to hell? "Been to hell and back" is an old expression that every one of us can relate to. Is there anyone who has *not* been to hell and back in his or her personal life? Not a single one, I think. Even Princess Diana, who lived a life most of us only dream of, experienced hell. But I'm asking if you've ever been to another kind of hell—a social hell, an economic hell, a demographic hell.

You say you've never been to hell?

I say, why not?!

Why haven't you been to hell? We aren't called to live in hell; we're called to live in heaven. But as Dante found out, you can't get to heaven without going through hell first.

The world is on fire—a world torn by hatred and strife, a world un-redeemed. A world that is God's worst nightmare, of which God can no longer speak these words: "And God saw that it was good."

Where are you getting singed? Where are you suffering for righteousness' sake? The Bible says, "Therefore, let those also who suffer according to the will of God entrust their souls to a faithful Creator in doing what is right" (1 Pet. 4:19). If you live as a Christian, you will suffer. When you live with integrity, you will suffer. When you live with honesty, you will suffer. When you live for justice, you will suffer.

So I ask you, what pain pierces your life right now because you bear the name "Christian," because you dare to walk through hell?

> The word came
> and he went
> in the other
> direction.
> God said: Cry
> tears of compassion
> tears of repentance; cry against
> the reek
> of unrighteousness; cry for
> the right turn
> the contrite spirit.
> And Jonah rose
> and fled
> in tearless
> silence.
>
> —THOMAS JOHN CARLISLE

Psalm 56:8 says, "You have kept count of my tossings; put my tears in your bottle. Are they not in your record?" (NRSV). The bottle of tears refers to an ancient practice of collecting one's tears and preserving them in a tear bottle made of glass, many of which had a bulbous bottom and a long neck flared at the top to facilitate collecting the tears. The chapel on the Mount of Olives known as Dominus Flevit, architecturally shaped like a tear bottle, is dedicated to Jesus weeping over Jerusalem. Some have even suggested that the woman who bathed Jesus' feet with her tears (Luke 7:38) was pouring out her bottle of tears. Where is our bottle of tears?

Here is a recent interview with a sharecropper's child in Selma, Alabama, by Raymond Wheeler of CBS-TV:

"Do you eat breakfast before school?"

"Sometimes, sir. Sometimes I have peas."

"And when you get to school, do you eat?"

"No, sir."

"Isn't there any food there?"

"Yes, sir."

"Why don't you have it?"

"I don't have the 35 cents."

"What do you do while the other children eat lunch?"

"I just sits there on the side" (his voice breaking).

"How do you feel when you see the other children eating?"

"I feel ashamed" (crying).

Is it right for one of the richest countries in the entire world to have such economic disparity that while some are breakfasting on caviar, others are going hungry?

Watching a "reality-based" crime program one evening, *Night Beat,* I watched a police briefing where the Newark chief of a narcotics unit tells his assembled officers not to "Be careful out there," but, "Remember, you are dealing with the scum of the earth." Does it make you cry when people spit in God's face and put themselves in God's place by treating those whom Jesus lived with, loved, and died for as the "scum of the earth"?

A science writer covering a National Institute of Health symposium on the potential super-drug "interleukin-12" reported that a representative of one of the involved companies, Genetics Institute, warned that: "The success of IL-12 against, say, leishmaniasis, at this point would be a disaster for

the company; G.I. [Genetics Institute] would be committed to scale-up man-
ufacturing, costing millions of dollars, and would probably wind up distrib-
uting the drug through the World Health Organization which would in
essence give it away, leaving the company with huge costs and little or no rev-
enues."

Does such a heartless attitude make you cry? Do you grieve over a world
that is going to hell in a shopping cart? Do you lament that consumerism is
the most virulent social disease ever to hit this planet?

A seasonal billboard perched above the doors of a Toronto strip club
recently read: "50 Luscious Babes to Tease and Please You. Open Good Friday."

Does such blatant sin make your blood boil?

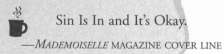 Sin Is In and It's Okay.

—*MADEMOISELLE* MAGAZINE COVER LINE

On July 1, 1996, ABC's *Good Morning America* ran a news story about
Chelsey Thomas, a young girl born without a smile because of a rare condition called Mobius syndrome. Her goal: to be able to smile by her eighth
birthday. More than anything in the world, she wanted to smile.

At the conclusion of the interview, the ABC reporter asked Chelsey, "You
know, a lot of people can smile but don't. They go around frowning. What
would you say to them?" To which Chelsey responded, "God gave you that
smile for a reason, so don't waste that gift by not using it."

"Tears trace an ancient hieroglyphic down your cheek,"
which (loosely translated) reads,
"Like it or not, life has got me by the nose and is taking me for a ride."

—HOWARD HANGER

I have a good friend named Sam. He is one of those older men who
brings wisdom to my life. One day we were talking about children—partic-
ularly how what we hope for our children and what our children actually do
with their lives often clash. We both agreed that as parents, we set ourselves
up for big-time hurt when we idealize the future of our children too much.

Sam slowly said, "You know, I've never told you this before, but I have a son who is thirty-four years old."

"Really? I never knew that," I responded.

"Yeah, he lives in Denver."

"Do you see him often?"

"I haven't seen him in a couple of years now."

"Why don't you see him?" I asked.

"Well, you see, he lives on the streets out there."

"What do you mean, he lives on the streets?"

"My son . . ." he said with a quivering lip, "my son, you see, is homeless."

Sam went on to explain a long and dramatic story of pain with this young man, and how they had tried to get him help. How they had depleted resources trying to help him. How they had been emotionally stretched like a guitar string to the point of breaking so many different times. How his last visit was so destructive that they had to decide the situation was out of their hands, that there was nothing more they could do as parents. Then Sam said, "We got to the point two years ago that we decided all we could do was to break all ties with him. But some nights . . . some nights, all I can do is lie in my bed and wonder where he is."

In all my years of ministry, I have never heard more parental pain. Where does that suffering come from? I finally have come to believe that suffering and love come from the same place inside our souls. If we did not love, there would be no suffering. We suffer and hurt and weep for our kids late into the night only because we love them and care about what happens to them. Sam hurt more deeply than any parent I've been around because he loved as much as any parent I've ever known.

Teach us to pray our tears, O Lord.
Absolve us of self-righteous pity
that our hearts might carry the burdens
which bring tears to your eyes.
Help us to cry beyond our own needs.
Receive our tears and transform them
into the cup of agape love Jesus poured out

before all humankind in need of healing drink.

—KARIN BACON

In 1996, a story appeared in *USA Today* written by columnist Susan Estrich about a crime committed by teenagers against a young girl. Here's the heart of the article:

What do you do with a 12-year-old murderer? According to police, the [perpetrator] and a group of kids kidnapped a 13-year-old, forced her into an abandoned, vermin-infested duplex, gang-raped and tortured her, barricaded the room, and then tried to set the house on fire to kill their victim and cover their tracks.

The duplex was next door to the bungalow where 82-year-old Viola McClain, known in Watts as "everybody's mama," had lived since 1935. McClain's 33-year-old grandson, Dumar Starks, smelled the smoke and confronted the two teenagers setting fire to the house. "We can do whatever we want to," they told him, and guns were drawn. "If you don't get out of the way, we'll smoke you."

Starks ran back inside. It was dusk, and his grandmother had just returned from church. She said, "Dumar, you can't change these people." Then she went out to the porch and was killed by a stray bullet.

For everything there is a season . . .
a time to weep, and a time to laugh.

—ECCLESIASTES 3:1, 4

Chapter 5
GOD IN OUR MIDST

The "Cold War" era was grim. Citizens of both the U.S. and U.S.S.R. were gripped by a frosty fear of everyone and everything, overshadowed by the specter of a mushroom-shaped cloud. Extreme paranoia did manage to give us, however, some great spy stories! This was the golden age for that golden guy "007," not to mention *The Man From U.N.C.L.E.*, *The Avengers*, *The Saint, Ice Station Zebra*, and *Mission Impossible*. Nothing seemed to stoke the imaginations of the spy-thriller genre like the chill of the Cold War. Secret agents and their wonderful, amazing, gravity-defying, usually exploding arsenal of secret weapons were the answer to everyone's insecurities.

Our fascination with "secret weapons" still runs strong. We remain convinced that some secret weapon will yet be developed that will put us in charge and keep us safe.

Centuries ago people looked to magic for their secret weapons. Amulets and incantations, special potions and rituals—all were humanity's secret weapons against the uncontrollable and uncontainable. Even the church was caught up in the power of mystical secret weapons against the perceived pow-ers of darkness. Before the Reformers turned the altar around, the mass was often understood as a big magic act. A remnant of this still resides in our lan-guage today. When a budding eight-year-old magician waves her plastic wand over a cardboard hat and declares "hocus-pocus," she is actually inton-ing an ancient sacred secret weapon. "Hocus-pocus" is a phrase derived from the Latin words the priest chanted as he raised the bread and wine into the incensed air. As the priest declared, "*Hoc est corpus meum*" ("This is my body"), he embodied the height of ecclesiastical alchemy—when matter became spirit. The highest drama of the week was ushered in by uttering that secret, sacred phrase that, when it reverberated around the massive nooks and crannies of medieval cathedrals, sounded more like "hocus–pocus" than "hoc est corpus meum."

The pre-Reformation church both had it right and had it wrong. It was right to recognize that the power of the Holy Spirit, the presence of the res-urrected Christ here on earth, was the greatest protective power a Christian could invoke. But it was wrong when its hierarchy tried to keep the gift of this presence a secret from the laity. Mark's Gospel presents this secret weapon—the gift of the Holy Spirit—in just the right way. The story is told of John the Baptizer who, in a loud booming voice to all who would hear his message, proclaimed: "Okay, now, this is no secret! Jesus is the Son of God, and he comes offering everyone who believes in him baptism in the Holy Spirit" (Mark 1:4–11).

When we receive Christian baptism, we all can lay claim to the most powerful secret weapon ever offered to creation—the power of God's love and grace made manifest within us. God's love is a transforming, transfigur-ing power so great that it has no comparison. The world still doubts this power because part of its "secretive" nature is its outward appearance. Who would think that a spirit described by the gospel writer and forever envi-sioned afterward by tradition as a "dove" would harbor such power?

If we are so miraculously empowered, why does the church continue to come across like some ninety-eight-pound wimp on the beach? Could it be because so few of us have taken this power, unleashed it, and released it into our lives? Most of us baptized in the Spirit are content to keep our secret weapon eternally caged up, never letting the Spirit test its wings in our world. In order to allow this secret weapon to function, we need to begin practicing what I call "power living." Just like bodybuilders and other serious athletes who commit a portion of every day to toning their muscles and strengthening their endurance, so Spirit-powered Christians must get into a daily regime to keep the power flowing. Power-living enables Christians to get "pumped up" with the Spirit.

Spiritual toning doesn't mean a visitation of some special spiritual gift every day of your life. What Spirit-powered living does involve is a commitment to a three-step practice that helps keep the wings of the Spirit beating strongly in your soul.

1.   Daily alignment with God and the sacred. Sunday morning just isn't enough. Spiritpowered living requires that we intentionally seek out God every day. There is no chance that familiarity with sacred ground will make it seem mundane. In fact, just the opposite is true. The more we seek to encounter the divine in our daily lives, the more we will begin to recognize that God's presence surrounds us and sustains us wherever we may be. Armed with that knowledge, we can be encouraged to pursue whatever task we are called to.

2.   Daily self-scrutiny and self-reflection. Everyone who has ever tried to tone a few muscles knows that isometric exercises— those that push our own muscles against each other—are the ones that build both tremendous strength and elasticity. Spirit-powered living turns the power of the Spirit inward as well as outward, creating deep reserves of energy and limitless wells of peace. Scrutinizing the motives and intentions behind all our actions and words enables us to let the Spirit of Christ within inform our every move. Gradually we build confidence in our own reactions and resources.

3.   Daily embodiment. This is Spirit-powered living in action. Christians must have both daily practices and daily games. The

Spirit that God lets free within our souls needs to be set free out in the world in order for its power to be fulfilled. But the strength of a Spirit-powered Christian isn't in a form recognizable to the secular world. The strength of the Spirit is in service.

We are God's people. We are not in the Secret Service; we are in the Spirit's service. Touched by the Spirit, we can think more clearly; feel more deeply; speak more truthfully; love more extravagantly; serve more creatively; give more lavishly; live more fully.

Where do you find the power to hang in there in this world?
Where do you find the power to keep going
when the going really gets tough?
Where do you find the power to continue
to believe in love in a world that is filled with hate?
Where do we find the power to continue to work for peace
in a world that is addicted to violence?
Where do we find the power to continue
to believe in good in a world that is filled
with so much suffering and pain?
Where do we find the power to continue
to believe that ultimately God's kingdom will come
and God's will, as revealed in Jesus, will be done in all of the creation?
Where do you find the power to be a disciple of Jesus in this world?

--JAMES A. HARNISH

The power comes from the Spirit of God, indwelling and empowering us. Elisabeth Elliot, in her book *A Lamp for My Feet,* said:

We cannot always or even often control events, but we can control how we respond to them. When things happen which dismay or appall, we ought to look to God for His meaning, remembering that He is not taken by surprise nor can his purposes be thwarted in the end. What God looks for is those who will worship Him in the midst of every circumstance. Our look of inquiring trust glorifies Him. This is our first responsibility: to glorify God. In the face of life's worst reversals and tragedies, the response of a faithful Christian is praise—not for the wrong itself, certainly, but for who God is and for the ultimate assurance that there is a pattern being worked out for those who love Him.

The only way to give up our fear and control issues to God is to spend time with the divine, the light that comes out of the darkness of what we can't possibly know or understand. As the psalmist said, "Be still, and know that I am God" (Ps. 46:10).

> We were meant to enjoy, to delight, to celebrate.
> To be fascinated by presence, mystery.
> To be wonder, amazement, surge of realization.
> To be so sensitive to patterns of beauty that they interest us and dwell in us
> from that time on.
> To be fully human is to have consummatory experience—
> when many lengths of experience come in conjunction
> and the worth of them hits us all at once.
> Instead of continuing to rush about,
> we take in, appreciate; we sense what it all means.
> We feel the flowing generosity of communion and consummation.
> The altogether lovely is present, not merely longed-for.
> We cleave to that which is good until we become one body with it.
> There are evils in the world which must be fought and problems which
> must be worked on. And they must not be ignored.
> But if our attention is constantly only upon them . . .
> we become eroded, rigid, drained of warmth, dehumanized.
>
> —ROSS SNYDER

There is a lot of romantic mush and nonsense written about the role of "silence" and "solitude" in the journey inward. New England poet May Sarton hits the reality check button with these powerful words:

I can tell you that solitude
Is not all exaltation, inner space
Where the soul breathes and work can be done.
Solitude exposes the nerve,
Raises up ghosts.

The past, never at rest, flows through it.

Ever notice how the places that are celebrated as "spiritual hot spots"—gifted with qualities that raise consciousness, enlighten the mind, bring peace to the soul—are located about as far away from where you are as possible? Popular spiritualists routinely tout the mountains of Tibet, the temples of India, or the deserts of New Mexico as the best locations for exalted spiritual insight and renewal. Perhaps that is one reason so many of us decide that setting out on a spiritual quest, going on a journey in search of God's perfect presence, is simply too much effort. Assuming that an experience of holiness requires some exotic, remote location, we despair of any hope of experiencing God in our own lives before we even get started.

Paul's speech before the Athenians in Acts 17 dared them to look at the evidence of the divine in their midst—not in their hundreds of futile shrines they had set up throughout the city, but on the monument to the "Unknown God," the itinerant preacher from Nazareth named Jesus. Knowing the unknown god, Paul declared, doesn't take an extended journey or clever philosophical argument. The truth, he revealed, had been present among them for a long time; God's design for humanity was outlined in God's creation and defined in the holy Scriptures.

Paul rejected the Athenians' vague searching for some unknown, out-of-sight god that remains forever evasive. The God Paul knew so well had not only been eternally close, but in fact, underfoot. In the person of Jesus Christ, God had become touchable, audible, and visible for every man, woman, and child. What, then, kept the Athenians from experiencing the truth of Jesus Christ—of God—in their midst? Why did Paul expose their search for the unknown god as a fruitless quest? Gary Hamel and C. K. Prahalad in their book *Competing for the Future* suggest that to move forward toward our goals, we must have a specific "strategic intent." The same is true for our spiritual quest as well. Without strategic intent we are just another generation wandering in the wilderness. But this intent doesn't mean trying every spiritual path or sipping from every spiritual cup offered our way. Intent depends, Hamel and Prahalad argue, upon the presence of three attributes in order for it to gain any headway.

A SENSE OF DIRECTION

Our spiritual journey gets off on the wrong foot when we make the mistake of looking for God's presence and purpose somewhere "out there." Instead of traveling off to some isolated mountaintop or deserted island, consider that Jesus spent the bulk of his spiritual journey, his earthly mission, in the ordinary towns and villages of his native Palestine. He taught and preached and performed miracles in the most humdrum of locations—in neighborhoods, at the docks, in homes filled with noisy kids and everyday chores.

Our faulty sense of direction tends to lead us far away from Jesus' focus of around and within. Instead of looking for God at our feet, in our homes, across our desks—we imagine the divine must be somewhere far away and out of reach. Instead of tuning in to the "still small voice" of God within, instead of "tuning our hearts to sing Thy praise," we bombard our hearts and souls with the blare of outside voices that demand from us first one loyalty and then another. As a result, we tend to lose our sense of direction altogether.

A SENSE OF DISCOVERY

The spiritual journey we each make is not simply a race to some cosmic finish line. The journey itself is as intentional as the destination. Esther Armstrong and Dale Stitt, founders of Journey Into Freedom ministry and authors of the newsletter by the same name, describe "journey" this way:

Inward journey brings us deeper into an intimate relationship with God, ourselves and others. Inward journey is about discovering our true self, who we are at the core. It is out of this search for truth and a deep relationship with God that we discover our call, our mission, where we are to invest our life energy.

When people live out of this deeper place, their depths, something profound happens to them. They are transformed. They become more authentic. They become persons of healing. They are good news. Hope, energy, peace flows from them into others. And while such people who live from a deeper place still have issues to address, challenges to meet, and problems to face, there is something different about them. There is a presence with them. A peace. A centeredness. . . . And we know they were not born this way. . . . all of them have been on a long, intentional, difficult, and sometimes lonely inner journey. They know that they will be on this inner journey for the rest of their lives.

Be open to the idea that the journey is not just a means to an end, the path to a goal. The journey is meaningful in and over itself. It is ongoing.

A SENSE OF DESTINY

Throughout his spiritual journey, Jesus moved with a clear sense of destiny—a focused passion of purposefulness. He sought to expose and explain God's matchless love to others, and as he moved toward his own personal destiny—the cross—his message became less about himself and more about the plan for our salvation. The closer Jesus came to God's presence, the more strongly the God within became evident to those around him.

Are you ready to set out on the greatest adventure, the most exciting journey of your life? There is nothing more exciting in life than to be a disciple of Jesus. Are you prepared to open yourself up to experiencing the God who is around and the God who is within?

> All our knowledge, sense and sight
> lie in deepest darkness shrouded
> till thy Spirit breaks our night
> with the beams of truth unclouded.
> Thou alone to God canst win us;
> Thou must work all good within us.
>
> --TOBIAS CLAUSNITZER

One thing that keeps many of us from experiencing God in our midst is the fear that his Spirit departs when darkness approaches. Yet the fact that God comes to us out of the darkness is a recurrent theme in the Scriptures. For many biblical characters, and for many of the early church's theologians, their positive experiences of God were primarily as darkness: unfathomable mystery, inexpressible presence. They could not penetrate the dark mysteries of redemption and resurrection, and did not pretend to. They reveled in the divine darkness. They embraced the fear of the Lord. They crossed the threshold of nothingness and discovered the soul's perfect freedom in the Cloud of Unknowing.

The Greek patriarchs developed most fully this notion that God is found profoundly in the darkness. Origen, in the early third century, pursued the image of Christ as shadow rather than light. In the fourth century Gregory of Nyssa presented the journey of faith as ascent from light to ever increasing darkness based on Moses' encounters with God on the smoking mountain. The fifth century Syrian named Dionysius bequeathed to us the beautiful phrase "ray of darkness." Perhaps one of the most misused and misunderstood phrases in the church today is by one of the greatest of Christian mystics, St. John of the Cross—"dark night of the soul." Pastors use it in their preaching and teaching to describe a phase of the soul that is the equivalent of "walking through the valley of the shadow of death," but St. John's "dark night" is neither a psychological nor pathological phase of the Christian life. It is his symbol for the entire journey of faith. "Those who enter the night never leave it, though the night changes."

John Wesley, founder of Methodism, once said the older he became, the more he came to see the inescapable darkness of our experience of God, indeed the essential nature of the experience of darkness in the spiritual life, and the closer he came to the position of St. John of the Cross. It is the dark of night that brings the light of day.

There is no pure daylight without the dark night.

One of the theologians I read while in seminary was Ladislaus Boros, who once wrote, "[Darkness] is perhaps the most distinctive and existentially most significant of the 'names of God.' God lives behind the 'clouds.'" The Welsh country doctor and poet Henry Vaughan wrote in words that have haunted Christians for centuries, "There is in God, some say, a deep but dazzling darkness."

According to Scripture, God came to us from out of the darkness. It was in the darkness that Love was consummated in the virgin Mary's womb; Jesus died upon a cross where "darkness came over the whole land until the ninth hour" (Mark 15:33 NIV); in the resurrection, Jesus was swathed in darkness. Darkness ushered the Messiah into the world, and darkness ushered the Messiah into eternity.

Where was God most revealed? Where is God most known? In the darkness atop Mount Sinai, of Bethlehem, of the Garden, of Calvary, and the grave. Then it should come as no surprise that God expects us to come to him in the darkness as well. It is no coincidence that God ordained the Hebrew Sabbath day to begin at sunset, when darkness swallows the daylight, when our senses are heightened and our need for God the greatest.

> It is when things go wrong, when the good things do not happen, when
> our prayers seem to have been lost, that God is most present. We do not
> need the sheltering winds when things go smoothly. We are closest to God
> in the darkness, stumbling along blindly.
>
> --MADELEINE L'ENGLE

Light was the first creation. When God wanted company in the universe, he created light. The unknown became known. Everything began in darkness. When there was nothing but God, there was only darkness (Gen. 1). On the first day God created light, then he separated the light from the primeval darkness and "called the light Day, and the darkness he called Night" (v. 5). The darkness gave birth to the light.

In the Christian tradition, revelation is understood as an experience of light. Light is God's self-communication. The difference between "God is nowhere" and "God is now here" is but the addition of a span, a space of light. Creation itself was the first self-revelation of God.

Put philosophically, darkness is nothing more than the absence of light; darkness is not caused except by the removal of light. Put scientifically, light only reveals things that are already there in the darkness. Light does not bring anything new, it only reveals things not seen before. Through light, things are shown in their relation to one another. Jesus, the Light of God, shows what is there all the time: a God who created us and who loves us with a passion. Through the light of Christ, God revealed the truth that we are meant for God. The light of God's face was Jesus Christ. Our only happiness, our true joy, is when God's light shines on us and we lift up "the light of [God's] countenance" on others (Ps. 4:6).

Light and dark constitute the essence of all the gifts through which God blessed his creation. Light and dark are twin manifestations of the divine workings in our lives. Both the day and the night belong to God: they are both the same with God. The language of the night is silence. The language of the day is speech. We need both.

To be a people of the light is to be a people of the night. Have you been blessed by the dark? Have you been blessed by the light? Can you say with T. S. Eliot, "I said to my soul, be still and let the dark come upon you, which shall be the darkness of God"? The God who is with us, the very God with us, is not just shedding light on us. God also sheds darkness. It is one thing to trust the God that you comprehend and understand; that's the God of light. It is quite another to trust and believe in the God beyond your comprehension and understanding. That's the God of the night. If all you can trust and have faith in is the God you can comprehend and understand, then who are you worshiping?

The knowledge of God is always a dark knowledge. Have you experienced the God of darkness? Have you submitted yourself to this darkness? It can work from deep within your being to bring you healing and strength, wholeness and hope.

> Have you been blessed by the dark?
> You are not your own.
> Have you been blessed by the light?
> You are not alone.

God is seen and yet not seen, known and yet unknown, even unknowable, revealed but always hidden and inscrutable.

Most of all, God is in our midst.

Chapter 6
CREATION: THE SOUND (SONG) OF GOD

> ⚜ Hear, that your soul may be healed.
> —ISAIAH 55:3 author's paraphrase

In twenty-first century terms, what are the building blocks of life? What is the essence of physical reality? Not chunks of matter, as modern science once thought, but pockets of energy, moments of experienced relationship.

I learned this personally the hard way. When I went to grade school in the late 1950s, I was taught that the smallest piece of matter was an atom; atoms were the building blocks of the universe. By junior high school in the 1960s, I learned that physicists had made a mistake. They had looked into an atom and discovered that it was basically empty space with something smaller inside—a nucleus. By the time I took physics in senior high school, physicists had looked into a nucleus and discovered that it, too, was basically empty space with something smaller inside—protons and neutrons. These were the real building blocks of the universe.

I waited until my senior year to take physics in college. By then I had learned that you can't trust physicists; they're always changing their minds, saying "Oops!" Thus it was not a total surprise when one day my professor at the University of Richmond instructed our class that physicists had once more looked into the heart of protons and neutrons, and guess what? They're basically empty space with particles inside called quarks and gluons. Every atom is a solar system in miniature. So quarks and gluons were truly the smallest building blocks of matter.

Is it any wonder I stopped taking physics? But some of my friends went on to study it in graduate school. Within a few years I was hearing that quarks were really empty space within which there is a particle zoo. To date, the quark "family" consists of twelve "fundamental particles"—six quarks and six leptons—surrounded by empty space. Who knows what may be discovered in a few more years!

Put simply, matter is composed of atoms, which are composed of empty space with a few particles inside. According to my physicist friends, there are only some 10^{80} particles in all the known universe. In fact, there are more fifty-note melodies to be generated from the eighty-eight keys of a piano keyboard than there are atoms in the entire universe. So why a solid wall? Not because of matter or particles, but because of electric fields between particles. Electric fields make matter corporeal and hold matter together. Want to know how little we all "matter"? If you took away all the empty space of everybody alive right now—all 5.75 billion of us—and gathered our matter together, it would fill the space of one large beach ball.

The complex relationships that exist between matter, energy, space, and time are the specialty of the Center for Non-Linear Studies at Sante Fe, where complexity science, the science of the future, is being generated. These "super-string physicists" contend that matter is nothing more than vibrating threads of energy, that you and I are the human organization of dancing energy. Sound is a function of vibrations, which give off frequencies. We hear something because we pick up its vibrations. Do you see brain waves? Do you see vibrations? No. But they are there. When God created you, God created you to be an unrepeatable, irreplaceable song. You don't have an atom in your body that isn't singing a song. Your genes, your ganglia, your liver, your lipids, every one of your cells vibrates.

> Sing lustily and with a good courage.
> Beware of singing as if you were half dead, or half asleep;
> but lift up your voice with strength.
>
> —JOHN WESLEY (1761)

So in spiritual terms the question is not, what are you made of, but what are you going to allow to occupy all that empty space? How little we matter, but how much our matter matters when it becomes inspirited!

But wait a minute: Haven't we heard this before?

> Open my ears, that I may hear
> voices of truth thou sendest clear;
> and while the wave notes fall on my ear,
> everything false will disappear.
> Silently now I wait for thee,
> ready, my God, thy will to see.
> Open my ears, illumine me,
> Spirit divine.
>
> —CLARA H. SCOTT (1895)

It's time we developed a theology of soundness, a "sound theology." The Greek word *cathecesis* is based on our word *echo*. As Christians, we should be an echo of God's voice. Could it be our theology isn't as solid as it should be because we haven't understood sound as a way of experiencing the divine? We don't "endure sound doctrine" because we don't "hold fast the form of sound words" (2 Tim. 4:3; 1:13 KJV) from the divine soundscape. Martin Luther insisted that God is a *deus loquens*—a "speaking God." Perhaps it is time to come to terms with the sonic realm of spirituality, such as the Gregorian chants of the Roman church, the Jesus Prayer chants of the Eastern Orthodox church, or the hymns of Protestantism.

It is the ear, not the eye, that is the "gateway to the soul." We would prefer the eyes over the ears because, as Lorenz Oken pointed out years ago, the eyes take us into the world whereas the ears take the world into us. Our ears are just powerful enough to develop a "hearing heart" and to discern God's voice. In fact, *discern* comes from the Hebrew word that means "to hear." The Schema really begins, not with "Hear, O Israel" but "Discern, O Israel: The Lord our God, the Lord is one. Love the Lord your God with all your heart and with all your soul and with all your strength."

Hearing is the first of the senses to greet us before we are born and the last of the senses to leave us at death. The "ear-gate"—so much more developed and sensitive than our "eye-gate"—has been created to act as the natural conduit between the Creator and all creation.

 How dull the forest would be if all bird—songs were the same?
—HANS PFITZNER'S OPERA, *PALESTRINA*

German philosopher and jazz musician Joachim-Ernst Berendt's path-breaking book *The World is Sound* (1987) is based on three questions: First, why has our sense of hearing been so carefully differentiated, much more so than our sense of seeing? Second, why are our ears given the "capacity for measuring," for the mathematical? Third, why are the data we receive from our ears so much more precise than that from our eyes?

The answer to all three of Berendt's questions lies in God's creation of our ears as altars for the presence and power of the living God, the place where God and man meet. From a biblical perspective, faith is not a "vision" thing, but a "vibration" thing. *Fides etauditu*, or in the words of the apostle Paul, "Faith comes by hearing, and hearing by the word of God" (Rom. 10:17 NKJV). From a deeply spiritual standpoint, you don't "see" a vision, you "hear" a vision. Sound becomes sight. Vibrations becomes visions. The invisible becomes visible. People who have perfect pitch hear in colors. Sound travels in waves and so does light. Speed up sound, or slow down light, and they are synonymous.

When asked how he came up with the design for his most famous residence, Fallingwater House in Bear Run, Pennsylvania, Welsh-American architect Frank Lloyd Wright replied, "The visit to the waterfall in the woods stays with me and a domicile has taken vague shape in my mind to the music of the stream."

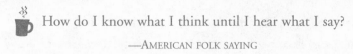

How do I know what I think until I hear what I say?
—AMERICAN FOLK SAYING

When hearing is good, speaking is good.
—ANCIENT EGYPTIAN PROVERB

Storytellers Stephen Spielberg and George Lucas have understood hearing as the essence of the soul for years. In the movie Jurassic Park, when did they first know that T-Rex was about to appear? Or in the Star Wars trilogy, how did Luke Skywalker learn to "use The Force"? Did he develop his powers of vision? Just the opposite. He was trained to suppress his natural inclination to "look" for The Force and instead "listen to" and "feel" it. How did you learn to drive a car? If you learned on a clutch, you went through the same training Luke Skywalker did. You learned amidst a lot of stalling out, grinding gears, and rolling backwards not to trust your eyes but to listen to the hum of the engine, the vibrations of the car, and to feel your way forward.

Chet Raymos, in his book *The Virgin and the Mousetrap*, says "cosmic vibrations are everywhere." From our cells to our cellular phones, from snowflakes to supernovas, everything emits vibrations, sounds to feed or famish our souls. A whole new academic field—acoustic ecology—is studying the sounds people listen to and finding ways to maximize the sounds people need and enjoy. Yet this is not a new idea. Paul the apostle knew that ,in order to interpret God, we must be able to discern the meaning of the sounds we hear (1 Cor. 14:10–11). What to some is the voice of God, to others is sheer noise. What to some is deafening thunder and lightning, to others is the voice of an angel (John 12:20–32). What to some is "bad luck" or "good fortune," to others is divine providence.

All music is gospel. All music is sacred.

We carve music up into categories for commercial reasons,
but really, that's just business.
All music is sacred because life is sacred.
We just need to live it.
—WILLIE NELSON

We used to talk about the silence of the deep oceans or the stillness of outer space. Now we know that all of creation hums with the sounds of life. Everything out there has a sound and rhythm, from otters and octopuses to quails and quasars. Fin whales can easily hear the bleeps of other fin whales four thousand miles away; some scientists argue, thirteen thousand miles away. Humpbacks often sing in rhyme, and the songs they sing are always changing. As they migrate the great oceans, males pass on their song to other males so that in any one season, all the whales in a single ocean will be singing the same song. Pythagoras, a Greek philosopher and mathematician, said, "A stone is frozen music." Jesus said that if we fail to praise him, the very stones will burst forth in song (Luke 19:40).

But wait a minute: Haven't we been singing this all along?

> This is my Father's world,
> And to my listening ears
> All nature sings, and round me rings
> The music of the spheres.
> This is my Father's world,
> the birds their carols raise,
> the morning light, the lily white,
> declare their Maker's praise.
> This is my Father's world:
> He shines in all that's fair;
> in the rustling grass, I hear Him pass;
> He speaks to me everywhere.
>
> —MALTBIE D. BABCOCK (1901)

Theologian Dorothee Solle once said, "In my opinion the two most important languages of humanity, theology and music, have the task of communicating precisely where other forms of communication are no longer possible."

Where is this in the Bible, you might ask? Let's start at the beginning. Note that the beginning of the Bible is a hymn, a creation hymn. Actually, one—third of the Bible is either poetry or hymn. Genesis 1 hymns how God created the world: "And God said, 'Let there be light' and there was light."

Creation was a spoken event. Creation was sounded forth, literally. Sound became sight. Cosmic vibrations became galactic visions.

Composer/conductor Leonard Bernstein, whenever he was conducting something from the Book of Genesis, argued that the best translation of the Hebrew was not "and God said," but "and God *sang*." For this reason the original Hebrew text of the Pentateuch was read aloud—or more accurately, chanted. In fact, it still is in some synagogues. In the monastic tradition, the *lectio divina* was read out loud because, as one heard the text and felt its vibrations, the monks believed the words would sound in the depths of one's being and the Bible's black letters would dance in the soul. The word *meditation* in Latin, *meditatio*, actually means "recitation." The meditation mantra "Amen" was the Christian's "Om."

Psalm 29, sung as a hymn, is explicit:

> The voice of the LORD is upon the waters;
> the God of glory thunders,
> The LORD, upon many waters.
> The voice of the LORD is powerful,
> the voice of the LORD is full of majesty.
> The voice of the LORD breaks the cedars,
> the LORD breaks the cedars of Lebanon.
> The voice of the LORD flashes forth flames of fire. . . .
> The voice of the LORD shakes the wilderness,
> the LORD shakes the wilderness of Kadesh.
> The voice of the LORD makes the oaks to whirl,
> and strips the forests bare;
> and in his temple all cry, "Glory!" (vv. 3–5, 7–9)

The Genesis creation still sounds even today, and scientists are picking up the soundings. In more romantic terms, the melody lingers on. According to the most recent scientific findings, sound waves may have helped shape how the cosmos was structured by orchestrating the pattern of galaxy clusters and huge voids seen in the night sky. Researchers like Alexander S. Szalay of Johns Hopkins University in Baltimore argue that acoustic oscillations (sound waves). given off when the universe was a cosmic soup and fog of protons and electrons, helped to structure the matter of the universe into galaxies and galaxy clusters. He and other scientists argue that the world is the creation of "acoustic waves," i.e., sound.

In Johannes Kepler's *Six-Part Harmony Motet*, the six visible planets with their elliptical orbits constitute the six-part harmony while the outer three planets add the rhythm section (in which Pluto beats the bass drum). Two researchers from Yale University—Willie Ruff and John Rodgers—put the "songs of the planets" into a synthesizer and made a recording of it ("The Harmony of the World"). David Deamer has composed a musical translation of DNA sequences he calls "DNA Music."

> The heavens declare the glory of God;
> And the firmament shows His handiwork.
> Day unto day utters speech,
> And night unto night reveals knowledge.
> There is no speech nor language
> Where their voice is not heard.
> Their line has gone out through all the earth,
> And their words to the end of the world.
>
> —PSALM 19:1–4 NKJV

It's a beautiful mystery that God created the world from sound, and the world sounds back praises to God. The cosmos is more than a random vibrational matrix. From the innumerable vibrations the cosmos could sing, it sings those vibrations that make "harmonic sense," and, ultimately, "musical sense." The electron shell of the carbon atom, physicists tell us, follows the laws of harmonics, producing the tone scale C—D—E—F—G—A. As Joachim-Ernst Berendt first pointed out, this is the hexachord of Gregorian chant. Could it be that all carbon-based life is actually built on the Gregorian chant? (Or is it the other way around?) It is more than a metaphor to say that every atom sings a song. The very nuclei of atoms make music.

In other words, the universe obeys the laws of harmonics. Scientists who are studying complexity now say that scientific findings are not so much meter readings or statistical discoveries as "resonances." For those engaged in the new scientific method, a scientific experiment results not in a formula, but in a resonance.

> With gratitude in your hearts sing psalms, hymns,
> and spiritual songs to God."
>
> —COLOSSIANS 3:16 NRSV

The four final hymns of the Book of Psalms have inspired musicians and composers throughout the ages, from Johann Sebastian Bach to Leonard Bernstein to Duke Ellington, to present their musical talent as an offering of thanks and praise to the Creator; can we do less? Let's begin seeing our lives in musical terms, by composing life from the inside-out rather than from the outside-in.

In some African tribes there is a singing ritual. The couple who is preparing for the birth of their child sit under a tree until a melody is heard which celebrates the coming of the child. While the infant is still in the womb and throughout the child's life, the parents sing this special song for him or her. They build life from the inside-out.

> The aim and final end of all music should be none other
> than the glory of God and refreshment of the soul.
> If heed is not paid to this, it is not true music but a
> diabolical bawling and twanging.
>
> —JOHANN SEBASTIAN BACH

Could it be that to sing is a sound thing to do? Literally? The story is told of the ancient Greek philosopher Pythagoras. As the shadows lengthened, he made his way down some narrow, cobblestone streets cradling his lyre and strumming on its strings the music of the spheres. Suddenly the light of a rising moon reflected a steely glint off the blade of a dagger wielded by an assassin hiding in a darkened doorway. With a blood-curdling scream, the man leaped from the darkness. Pythagoras whirled to face his assailant. Instead of meeting him in mortal combat, Pythagoras began to play a piece of music on the lyre. The haunting strains cut deep into the soul of the would-be assassin. He dropped the knife and fell sobbing to his knees, overcome in a torrent of emotion that swelled from the depths of his soul.

Songs are more than barometers that record atmospheric pressure without being able to do anything to change the weather itself. Songs are less a consequence than a cause of events. The kind of songs our souls sing affects our world and affects our health. The ability of music to affect the body is only beginning to be understood. Our beings are bathed in vibrations that may very well set the tone and tune of our lives.

But wait a minute: Haven't we been singing this all along?

> Down in the human heart, crushed by the tempter,
> Feelings lie buried that grace can restore.
> Touched by a loving heart, wakened by kindness,
> Chords that are broken will vibrate once more.
> —FANNY CROSBY (1869)

It wasn't only the blind hymn writer Fanny Crosby who testified to the healing power of music. The original meaning of the Latin word *cantare*, from which we get our English word "to sing," meant "to work magic" or "to heal." *Carmen*, the Latin word for "poem," originally meant "magic formula." Finally a cantor became someone who worked magic, who worked healing, with sounds or music. A "cantata" was a healing piece of music.

Music can heal or harm. Negative music creates negative states of consciousness, hence the dangers of "gangsta" rap, hard-core punk, grunge, or heavy metal in creating "harmonic clash"—a condition we experience when we find the rhythm of our souls out of harmony with the resonance of God's universe. If music is, at base, a set of vibrations called the harmonic series, as Leonard Bernstein insisted, then certain harmonic forms create and connect with certain emotions and moods and personalities. Music is moving because it conjures the passions; it makes us feel an emotion or sensation. One is moved by music because, according to Aaron Ridley, it arouses in us a passionate response which is sympathetic, empathetic, and associative.

> The earth sings MI, FA, MI so that you may
> infer even from the syllables that in this our
> domicile MISERY and FAMINE obtain.
> —JOHANN KEPLER

Japanese mathematician/research scientist Susumu Ohno translated a funeral march by Chopin from notes into chemical equations. He found the entire passage was almost identical to a cancer gene found in humans. Perhaps Leo Tolstoy was more right than he knew when he saw the connection between music and the body: "Music is the shorthand of the emotions," and the "emotions are the bridge between the mental and the physical."

Listen to Tchaikovsky's Sixth Symphony without getting depressed. Listen to Chopin's Funeral March without getting sad. Listen to Beethoven's Fifth Symphony without feeling joy. In Johann Sebastian Bach's Mass in B Minor there are seven basic keys to the harmonic, hieratic schemes of human emotions: E minor is the crucifixion key; B minor, the key of human pain; G major is blessedness; C major is contentment; A major is joy and grace; F and C-sharp minor are transcendent suffering; and D major is triumph, worldly power, and glory. Bach is a master at playing the strings of the heart.

> If you ask me tomorrow or any other day why
> some sounds are sad and others glad, I shall
> not be able to tell you. Not even your Papa
> could tell you that. Why, what a thing to ask,
> my pets! If you knew that, you would know
> everything. Good night, my dears, good night.
>
> —Rebecca West

Welsh English physician Ernest Lloyd used to lecture his students in the mysteries of the heart. He would crescendo the heart's wonders until he dropped to a whisper: "Have you ever heard a mitral murmur, boys, have you? It's like the wind rustling through the golden corn. You think I'm being poetic? Why, when you listen with your stethoscope to the old heart, boys, you are listening to a kind of poetry."

That old Welsh doctor didn't know how right he was. "Soundprints," or sonograms, are made by a computer breaking your voice down into intervals a thousandth of a second long, each interval containing thousands of frequencies of sound which the computer lays out on a graph. Recently, researchers at Beth Israel Hospital in Boston have taken soundprints one step further. They have discovered that every heartbeat gives off certain frequencies that are totally unique. Called "heart songs," one of the researchers has hired a composer to put his own "heart song" into symphonic form.

But wait a minute: Haven't we been singing this all along?

> There's within my heart a melody
> Jesus whispers sweet and low:
> Fear not, I am with thee, peace, be still,
> In all of life's ebb and flow.
>
> —Luther B. Bridgers (1910)

We've always suspected this to be the case. In fact, we've even devised a language for it. When the "constellation" of vibrating energies between two people move toward one another—in all their juxtapositions and oppositions—and those vibrations are in sympathy with each other, we say two people are "on the same wavelength" or are "in tune with each other," or they "make beautiful music together" or give off "good vibes." When the constellation of vibrations do not match, we say two people are "not on the same wavelength," or they give off "bad vibes."

> You offer me flowers, yet I can live without flowers and
> many other things as well. But one thing I cannot and
> will not do without: I can never live as much as a single
> day in which the music in my heart is not dominant. If I
> am to live with a man, it must be one whose inner music
> harmonizes with mine, and his single desire must be that
> his own music be pure.
>
> —Herman Hesse's "Iris"

Soldiers throughout history have known about sympathetic vibrations, as have certain opera singers like Caruso and jazz musicians like Ella Fitzgerald. Before soldiers cross a bridge, they break step. Why? Because their cadence gives off a frequency, a sound. If their marching song matches the frequency of the bridge, then there is achieved a technical state called "resonance," in which there is a tremendous explosion of energy. Something's got to give, and it isn't going to be the song! Whether the bridge is built of stone or steel, that song bombs the bridge and essentially blows it up.

You still don't think vibrations have power?

What accompanied the ark as it was brought into Jerusalem (2 Sam. 6:15)?

What brought down the walls of Jericho (Josh. 6:15–20)?

What recently collapsed the Tacoma bridge? The wind created a double oscillation that matched the frequency of the bridge, and it came crashing down.

Why is it forbidden to sing "Louie, Louie" at a Clemson football game? Because a few years ago the stadium began to crumble. University officials discovered it wasn't because of defective architectural design or inferior construction work or materials; it was because the song "Louie, Louie" gave off frequencies that perfectly matched the frequency of the stadium.

Now, can you understand why prayer—the Christian's soul-song—is the most powerful force in the universe, especially when two or more are gathered together in Christ's name?

> Our Father
> Who art in heaven,
> Hallowed be Thy name.
> Thy kingdom come, Thy will be done,
> On earth, as it is in heaven.
> Give us this day our daily bread,
> And forgive us our trespasses
> As we forgive those who trespass against us.
> And lead us not into temptation,
> But deliver us from evil.
> For Thine is the kingdom, and the power, and the glory, forever.

The Lord's Prayer, as taught by Jesus in Matthew 6, is really the prayer Jesus gave his disciples to pray. We can call it "The Lord's Prayer" only if the point is not to say it but to become it. Our greatest ambition in life should be to become a Lord's "pray-er," to have everything we think, say, and do be dedicated and offered to God as a prayer of sacrifice and praise.

So this is prayer: Turn Off, Turn On, Tune In, Fine-Tune, and Stay Tuned. First, prayer is when our souls turn off the frequencies of the world and all its static and dissonance. Second, prayer is turning on to the frequencies where God's Spirit operates and not allowing other registers to lure us away. Third, prayer is tuning in to those frequencies of the Spirit where love holds sway. Jacob Boehme said the soul itself is "a tuned instrument of the harmony of God," a part of God's kingdom of joy "which God's Spirit would play upon."

Fourth, prayer is tuning up our souls through constant fine-tuning to the music of the spheres. We can do this because God gave us a tuning fork to the eternal, God's perfect pitch: Jesus, the Christ. Finally, when we "stay" our lives tuned into his song, we—individually and as the body of Christ, the church—can experience resonance with the eternal.

But wait a minute: Haven't we been singing this all along?

> Come, thou Fount of every blessing,
> tune my heart to sing thy grace;
> streams of mercy, never ceasing,
> call for songs of loudest praise.
> Teach me some melodious sonnet,
> sung by flaming tongues above.
> Praise the mount! I'm fixed upon it,
> mount of thy redeeming love.
> —ROBERT ROBINSON (1758)

When resonance is reached, something's got to give, and it's not going to be God! When we vibrate with the eternal, we become transformed into God's image and take on the likeness and consciousness of Christ. In these high moments of resonance, there is such an unleashing and releasing of resurrection energy that we become the Lord's Prayer: We allow God's melody to shape us, and, in turn, we shape others for God's kingdom.

> Look around you.
> We are the notes and the melody of your opus.
> We are the music of your life.
> —PATRICK SHEANE DUNCAN'S MR. HOLLAND'S OPUS
> [God] needs us as a conductor for his choir,
> for the performance of an unending music.
> —R. S. THOMAS

Chapter 7
PRAYER: MORE THAN A ZEN THING

Novelist, essayist, poet, dramatist, and rancher Gertel Ehrlich (b. 1946) became interested in Zen when she was required to attend chapel at her boarding school. She snuck Zen master D.T. Suzuki's writings into her hymnal, and during what she calls the "go-to-church Christian regime" of cerebral exercises, she tutored herself in the practices of Zen.

"I've always had the need to experience things in my body," she says. Struck by lightning twice, Ehrlich is now writing about how one is different after a million volts of electricity course through one's body.

Who will tell her one is different after experiencing the power of God's love and grace? Who will explain to her British poet Kathleen Raine's line, "But once is enough to know forever?"

In our life-on-the-edge culture, Zen is becoming ever popular due to its "experience-based" emphasis—its primary exercise of meditation is said to bring soothing peace and enhanced sensual and intellectual stimulation into the life of the practitioner. In a Zen state, one can raise and lower body temperature, alter pulse rate, even induce "spiritual encounters." Prayer on the other hand, though meditative in essence, is more than elevating one-self—one's body, one's spirit—to a higher spiritual plane. It is communication with the highest spiritual level in the universe: God. Not a punch list or demand letter for the Almighty to fulfill (much to the dismay of faith-force believers and on-the-fringe agnostics who would convert with just one more miracle), it is a means of getting to know God personally and having direct conversation with the Creator on a one-on-one basis.

Far too often, however, we Christians spend our prayer time praying our way out of trouble instead of praying ourselves into the will of God.

The things, good Lord, that I pray for, give me your grace to labor for.
—THOMAS MORE

Now there were certain Greeks . . . [who] came to Philip . . . and asked him, saying, "Sir, we wish to see Jesus. . . . But Jesus [said], "The hour has come that the Son of Man should be glorified. Most assuredly, I say to you, unless a grain of wheat falls into the ground and dies, it remains alone; but if it dies, it produces much grain. He who loves his life will lose it, and he who hates his life in this world will keep it for eternal life. If anyone serves Me, let him follow Me; and where I am, there My servant will be also. If anyone serves Me, him My Father will honor.
"Now my soul is troubled, and what shall I say? 'Father, save Me from this hour?' But for this purpose I came to this hour. Father, glorify Your name."
Then a voice came from heaven, saying,
"I have both glorified it and will glorify it again."
Therefore the people who stood by and heard it said that it had thundered.
Others said, "An angel has spoken to Him."
Jesus answered and said, "This voice did not come because of Me, but for your sake. Now is the judgement of this world; now the ruler of this world will be cast out. And I, if I am lifted up from the earth, will draw all peoples to Myself."
—JOHN 12:20–32 NKJV

In these verses, John gives us a scene that has no parallel in any of the other Gospels. Following on the heels of a dispute among the Pharisees, "Look, the world has gone after Him" (v. 19), John notes the arrival of some Greeks who voice their desire to "see Jesus." The fact that these Greeks have apparently gone up to worship at the temple during the Passover festival and that they are interested in seeing the now notable Jesus indicates that these men are either "God-fearers" (Torah-observers but not circumcised) or full proselytes to Judaism.

Instead of confronting Jesus directly, however, these men first seek out Philip to pull some strings. Eventually Philip, along with Andrew, goes to Jesus and announces the Greeks' request. But instead of focusing on what these seekers wanted, John's text dumps them and never refers to them again. Their purpose was chiefly to backdrop the declaration Jesus makes next before his disciples. Although the Greeks themselves disappear from sight, they usher in a new age, a time when "the hour has come" for the Son of Man to "be glorified." The appearance of the Greek proselytes defines a crucial moment in Jesus' ministry.

Obviously, John is not concerned that Jesus directly answer the Greeks' request for an audience. His concern is that if these Greeks must "see" to believe, then they had better "see" the right Jesus. Not the Jesus whose reputation as a great teacher, healer, and miracle worker had gained him a burgeoning ministry, but the Jesus whose hour of glorification had come, and would be fulfilled through abandonment, suffering, and death. Only there could his real mission be understood.

But Jesus does not stop there He continues on to offer yet another lesson on discipleship. Like himself, his disciples must be willing to follow God's plan to the end, even death itself, if they are to "bear fruit." This leads John to the very core of discipleship: whoever would save his or her life will lose it, but whoever would lose his or her life (for the sake of the gospel) will find it. The call to discipleship is a call to sacrifice (goals and ambitions, comfort and luxury), to suffer, perhaps even to die for others, in order to live as God intends us to live, to live as Jesus did. This unexpected nature of messiahship and discipleship—one that embraces servanthood and dying to self—is not an easy pill to swallow, not even for Jesus. In fact, he admits that his soul is "troubled" by the sacrificial death that looms in his future. But now is not the time to draw back or try to sidestep his messianic future.

Some scholars suggest that the Greeks mentioned in this passage of John's Gospel are a kind of final temptation to Jesus before he heads down the Passion path. Might they not represent the lure of a Gentile mission that Jesus could turn toward at this time, instead of continuing his clashing charge among the "Jews" and its tragic outcome? Or perhaps they represent the temptation of continuing a wildly successful mission among Jews and Greeks? The possibilities of an earthly ministry lasting another ten, twenty years are endless and incredible!

Yet there is no evidence that these thoughts crossed Jesus' mind. Rather, he fully accepted the terms of his messianic identity. His obedience mirrors the call to discipleship Jesus extended to others. He refuses to try to save himself. Instead, he calls to God to "glorify Your name" (John 12:28). In confirmation, the voice from heaven responds directly to Jesus' obedience, affirming his understanding both of his identity and his future. While this voice is not quite a private communication with Jesus, it is decidedly not clarified for the general crowd. Though John's text suggests that all gathered nearby heard something, there is considerable disagreement over what that something was.

For some, the message of a suffering servant, a crucified Christ, a mortal Messiah, was beyond the pale of their comprehension; so for some who witnessed the heavenly voice's response to Jesus' obedience, the message is impenetrable. For a great many, Jesus' teachings remained scrambled, turning whole notions of messianic leadership, divine power, and glorification over hard and on their heads. To those who simply cannot "get it," the voice is only so much noise—the din of thunder. To a handful, however, those who had listened to Jesus' teachings and heard his call to discipleship and service and had begun to grasp it, the heavenly voice sounded like that of an angel. Though they could not yet discern the whole implication of what was to come, they sensed the presence of the divine in their midst.

Divine, yes, but fully human as well. How did he get through those next few months, knowing they would end in misery and death? He prepared himself for the "coming" hour . . . through prayer.

Johann Sebastian Bach was not the first composer/artist/author to write on a finished work, above or below his own name, the initials "AMDG." The initials were Latin shorthand for the phrase, "Ad Majorem Dei Gloria," which translated means "For the Greater Glory of God Alone."

For far too many of us, there are only two attitudes toward prayer—those who "pray their way in," and those who "pray their way out." Most of us, unfortunately, take our prayer lives most seriously when we are trying to "pray our way out":

- When you're rushing to get to an appointment that you're already late for and you don't notice the traffic cop's car until you've whizzed halfway past it—time to "pray your way out."

- When you walk into math class and suddenly realize the chapter test is today, not tomorrow—time to "pray your way out."

- When you get a letter with a return address from the Internal Revenue Service—time to "pray your way out."

- When your company announces it will begin downsizing/"right-sizing"/"upsizing" or whatever else they call it—time to "pray your way out."

- When your spouse confronts you with the possibility of divorce—time to "pray your way out."

Life hits a skid when situations arise that may cause pain or fear, anger or hardship. We are suddenly brought up short. Even those who might not consider themselves very pious or prayerful, or even very religious, when faced with these kinds of clutch circumstances, hurl up "panic-button prayers"—they pray to God for help in getting out of the messes they've landed in.

One has to wonder whether God doesn't spend the better part of the day hearing attempts by people to "pray their way out" of situations. It must get very old. Praying-one's-way-out prayers are not very creative or new. When we're trying to pray our way out, there simply isn't time to be eloquent. I know that Jesus listens to my panic-button prayers because he himself got to a point in his life where he authored and offered one of the classic "greats" in this genre of praying: "Father, get me out of here!" As he looked down the road toward Jerusalem, he cried out, "Father, save me from this hour" (John 12:27).

Sometimes we try to dress up our panic-button prayers by gilding them with flowery promises. We promise we'll never speed, slack, cheat, lie, or steal ever again if God will just get us out of this one. As if God hasn't heard that before. But there is another kind of attitude Christians can take in prayer. Instead of flailing around for an escape hatch, instead of praying our way out, we can "pray our way in" to God's plan for our lives.

- Confronted with the need to make a mid-life career change—trust God's plan and *pray your way in* to a new possibility.

- Finding that the demands on your time are causing your blood pressure to rise, your head to pound, and your nerves to snap—trust God's plan and *pray your way in* to a slower pace.

- Discarding another commodity of fun for a community of faith that can nurture your soul while prodding you forward—trust God's plan and *pray your way in* to a new address.

- Worried about the strain on your budget and hating the pinched feeling you always have at the end of the month—trust God's plan and *pray your way in* to a new examination of what is an authentic style of life and what is just "lifestyle."

- Grieving over the loss of a spouse—trust God's plan and *pray your way in* to a renewed love for family and friends.

Much of life is beyond our control. We can't run the show, so we might as well relax and enjoy the picture. Why don't we trust God's plan and *pray our way in* to a yielded life?

A few years ago, Henry Blackaby challenged the Christian community to rethink its approach to God. In his now-classic discipleship resource, *Experiencing God,* Blackaby pointed out that our approach to God most resembles a Christmas wish list—a litany of blessing "gimmes" that itemizes what we want: "Lord, bless our church, bless my family, bless my ministry, bless my hopes, bless my dreams, bless my desires." Blackaby proposed following Jesus' lead and learning to pray not for what we want but for what God wants for us. Instead of asking God to bless our lives, authentic discipleship is asking God to "Let my church, my family, my ministry, my hopes, my dreams, my desires be a part of what you are blessing."

Mother Teresa used to talk about shifting our prayers from what we want to what God wants. In John 12, Jesus shifts the direction of our prayers even further. Instead of asking God to "save me from this problem," or "deliver me from this mess/stress/distress," Jesus teaches us to ask God to "glorify Your name" in this action. When God's voice rang down out of heaven and promised that he was, in fact, being glorified, some heard angel voices while others heard thunder. When your life takes unexpected turns, crashes into a barren spot, or overwhelms you with responsibility, do you hear the din of thunder roaring in your ears? Or do you hear the voice of an angel offering you a chance to glorify God?

It's your choice. Either you can try to pray your way out of a thunderstorm, or you can pray your way in to the glory of God.

> Prayer that craves a particular commodity . . . is vicious.
> Prayer as a means to effect a private end is meanness and theft. . . .
> As soon as man is at one with God, he will not beg.
> He will then see prayer in all action.
> The prayer of the farmer kneeling in his field is to weed it.
>
> —Ralph Waldo Emerson

These latter days of the twentieth century are filled with background noises and subliminal forces that speak in shouted whispers, "Don't breathe in." A spirituality for the twenty-first century begins with an experience of aliveness and deep breathing of life. After all . . .

Jesus took a deep breath when he chose Simon the Zealot as a disciple, and political barriers were blown away.

Jesus took a deep breath when he dined with Zacchaeus the despised publican, and class barriers were blown away.

Jesus took a deep breath when he conversed with a woman of Samaria, and sexual barriers were blown away.

Jesus took a deep breath when he celebrated a Roman centurion's faith, and racial barriers were blown away.

Jesus took a deep breath when he allowed a woman who was a sinner to touch him, and ideological barriers were blown away.

Jesus took a deep breath when he praised a poor widow who offered her mite, and economic barriers were blown away.

Jesus took a deep breath when he heeded the appeal of a Syro-Phoenician woman, and national barriers were blown away.

Jesus took a deep breath when he washed his disciples' feet, and social barriers were blown away.

Jesus took a deep breath when he rebuked his disciples for criticizing a follower who was an outsider of the group, and denominational barriers were blown away.

Jesus took a deep breath when he chastised the adults for not suffering the children to come unto him, and ageist barriers were blown away.

Jesus took a deep breath when he told Lazarus to come forth, and physical barriers were blown away.

Jesus, God's breath made flesh, took deep breaths—Will we? Will we be God's breath made flesh?

 Let everything that breathes praise the Lord
—HEBREW PSALMIST

To help you get in touch with God's breath within you, follow these deep-breathing exercises to improve your spiritual fitness:

1.   Close your eyes and think of a tennis court. The total surface area of your lungs is roughly the size of a tennis court, providing enough space for some three hundred billion capillaries. If stretched from end to end, these capillaries would reach from New York to Florida.

2. Take the breath of life. You are that one breath away from eternity. Every twenty-four hours you are 23,240 one-breaths away from eternity. God is constantly pouring out puffs of life into you, life that is that fragile.

3. Listen to yourself breathe the breath of life. Every twenty-four hours you breathe in some twenty million particles of foreign matter (if you live in an urban area). Our ancestors also breathed in polluted air, although not to the extent that we do. Carbon deposits from inhaling wood smoke in unventilated dwellings are commonly found in the lungs of preserved mummies. God made those billions of capillaries to help rid the lungs of foreign matter.

4. Breathe in a large amount of oxygen and hold it. Thirty-five percent of the oxygen molecules we inhale in one breath comes from the rain forests, which we are chopping down at a rate of twenty-five million hectares a year. Every minute, four football fields of forests disappear from the face of the earth. Every minute, two hundred football fields of arable land disappear under concrete. Breathe out a prayer of repentance.

5. Holding someone's hand, take a deep breath of life. Nothing is more personal and private than breathing, yet nothing connects us more to one another and the earth. Each breath we take contains approximately a quadrillion (10^{15}) atoms already breathed by the rest of humanity within the past few weeks.

6. Take another deep breath. The connectedness of our breathing encompasses not simply the human order, but all creatures that breathe, including persons, plants, and animals.

7. Stand in front of a picture of a family member who has died. Recall joyful memories of them and laugh. With the breath you

took for that laugh, your loved one literally became a part of you. In every breath there are more than a million atoms breathed personally at one time or another by every breathing earthling that has ever lived.

8. Breathe meditatively. The breath-taking, nay, breath-giving truth of aliveness is more than Methuselean in its span: part of your body right now was once actually, literally, part of the body of Abraham, Sarah, Noah, Esther, David, Abigail, Moses, Ruth, Matthew, Mary, Luke, Martha, John, Priscilla, Paul . . . and Jesus.

9. Keep breathing quietly. You have within you not just the powers of goodness resident in the great biblical characters like Moses and the Lord Jesus. You also have within you the forces of evil and destruction. The youthful comrade and confidant of Joan of Arc was Gilles de Rais, a marshall of France and one of the wealthiest men in Europe, who was condemned to the stake in 1440 for the crimes of witchcraft, heresy, sodomy, and the sexual abuse and the murder of over 140 children. Resident in each breath you take is the body of angels like Joan of Arc and devils like Gilles de Rais, Genghis Khan, Judas Iscariot, Herod, Hitler, Stalin, Pol Pot, and all the other destructive spirits throughout history.

Breathe on Me, Breath of God

Chapter 8
ANCIENT/FUTURE FAITH AND HOPE

In the early days of the Tennessee Valley Project (TVA), a dilapidated log homestead had to be abandoned to make room for a lake behind the dam. A new home on the hillside had already been erected for the cabin's poor Appalachian family, but they refused to move into their beautiful new split-level ranch ("splanch," as they called it).

The day of the flooding arrived, but still the family refused to move. As the bulldozers were brought in, the Appalachian family brought out their shotguns. No amount of legal brandishings or bulldozer menacings would budge this family from their cabin.

Then someone from the TVA decided to try one last-ditch effort to end the stalemate. They called in a social worker to talk with the family and find out what their problem was. "We ain't goin' anywhere," the family announced to the social worker. "Nobody can make us. We're not budging no matter how many threats you make or how rundown our li'l cabin may look to you!"

The social worker pleaded, "Help me to explain to the authorities why you won't move into your beautiful new home."

"See that fire over there?" the man asked, pointing to a blazing fire in the primitive hearth of the log cottage. "My grandpa built that fire over a hundred years ago," the man explained. "He never let it go out, for he had no matches and it was a long way to a neighbor's. Then my pa tended the fire, and since he died, I've tended it. None of us ever let it die, and I ain't a-goin' to move away now and let grandpa's fire go out!"

This gave the social worker an idea. She arranged for a large apple butter kettle to be delivered to the home. She explained to the family that they could scoop up the live coals from the fire and carry them to the new home where they would then be poured out and fresh kindling added. In this way grandpa's fire need never go out. Would this be acceptable?

This Appalachian family huddled, and then agreed to move from their shack in the hollow to the new home on the hillside. But they wouldn't budge—until they could take with them the fire of their ancestors.

The past is important because it gives us comfort and hope in the present. But it should also give us direction for the future. A Native American tribe, the Swampy Cree Indians, begin their stories about their tradition with the phrase, "I go backward, look forward, as the porcupine does." The phrase comes from the Cree description of a porcupine as he backs into a rock crevice: *Use puyew usu wapiw.* Translated, it literally means "he goes backward, looks forward."

As Howard A. Norman puts it in his introduction to *The Wishing Bone Cycle,* "The porcupine consciously goes backward in order to speculate safely on the future, allowing him to look out at his enemy or the new day."

Like the porcupine, to move ahead in life we must first find a rock crevice and go backward. Before our souls move forward, we must make sure to take the fires of our ancestors with us. But how?

The Issachar Window is one of the most stunning of Marc Chagall's twelve Jerusalem Windows, which grace the synagogue at the Hadassah Hospital in Jerusalem. The tribe of Issachar was an agricultural tribe that worked hard and reaped an abundance from its labors with the soil. The Bible says Issachar's people loved their land so much that they would not leave it, even to go to war (Gen. 49:14–15). Tradition also has it that Zebulun and Issachar made a pact between them: Zebulun would enter the commercial arena to allow Issachar the time to spend in scholarship and study of the Torah. Hence the gift the Issachar tribe gave to David was this: we are the people who "had understanding of the times, to know what Israel ought to do" (1 Chron. 12:32).

A journalist once asked Wayne Gretsky, arguably the greatest hockey player who ever lived, what his secret of success was. Gretsky replied, "I just skate to where the puck is going to be."

What if the church were to raise up some leaders who could be a people, like the sons and daughters of Issachar, who know the times and know what to do? It doesn't do any good to know what the signs of the times are unless you know what to do about them.

What are the signs of our times?

We get our soft drinks in high-tech plastic bottles, but we've brought back the classic curves. We have digital cameras that capture lifelike color, while black and white photography is making a comeback. We have wide-screen, surround-sound TVs so that those classic movies from the '30s and '40s will seem as big as life. We're sensing a longing for the old and the familiar even as time hurtles forward toward the threshold of a new millennium.

These are just a sprinkling of the signs of the times.

These are the reasons why we need ancient/future faith. Faith that's filled with new/old thinking, that reappropriates the traditional into the contemporary. Faith that mingles the old-fashioned with the new-fangled and understands the times in which we live, in order to claim the era in which God has placed us for Jesus Christ.

To those for whom a steady stream of public complaint against the postmodern culture has become a cottage industry, it's time we heard the words: "Get over it"—then "Get ahead of it"!

If the church is to "get ahead of it," then it can learn a great deal from author/futurist Faith Popcorn. From the perspective of Malcolm Muggeridge, Faith Popcorn's book *Clicking*, her sequel to *The Popcorn Report*, deserves the death dismissal, "Get thee behind me, Satan." But from the perspective of futurist Marshall McLuhan, Popcorn's attempt to get people and

organizations to "future-fit" rather than "retro-fit" their lives and their thinking constitutes a very present help in a time of trouble. In fact, *Clicking*
might also be called, *How to Get to the Future Before the Future Gets to You.*
Here are a few of the indicators she's picked up on:

Foods of the future? Better like mixed metaphors, like pizza burritos,
Thai salsa, and Tex-Mex egg rolls.

Diet Sodas? Declining.

Fastest growing snack? Beef jerky.

Butter sales? Booming at levels rivaling thirty years ago.

Households having unlisted phone numbers? One in five, or 20 million.

Largest single source of food in the world? McDonald's.

Fastest growing recreational sport in America? In-line skating.

One of the highest indicators of high income level? The higher your
regard for family values and quality family time.

How Rush Limbaugh found his true love? E-mail.

Amount of money pet owners spend annually on pet toys? Two hundred
and ten dollars.

Percent of American households with personal computers? Thirty-eight
percent.

Newest competitor in the wedding industry? Disney's theme park wed-
dings.

What Popcorn does better than other professors of the future is take
things you and I do naturally and normally, give them a name, and then
show how what we're doing fits into a larger cultural scenario. "What we're
trying to do by detailing the trends," says Popcorn and her coauthor, Lys
Marigold, "is to force you to think differently. Find new patterns in things.
Question the obvious. Because *clicking* is about breaking cliches, ripping
apart refrigerator door philosophy—comforting words to live by that don't
necessarily hold true anymore."

Ever turn off the TV because a program is too violent? You've joined the
rank of . . . *click* . . . "Vigilante Consumer."

Women, have you bought a car recently, possibly from a woman sales-
person? Over 50 percent of all new cars sold in the U.S. are bought by

women, a figure that is climbing to 60 percent as we approach the "millennium of the woman." *Click* . . . "Female Think."

Men, have you seen any of these movies—*To Wong Foo, Mrs. Doubtfire, The Crying Game*—or found yourself crying in public ("I love you, man!"), or been to a Promise Keepers event? *Click* . . . "Mancipation."

Do you find yourself doing many things at once, but sometimes getting so frustrated by "beeper bondage" that you turn off all your machines and simply detach? *Click* . . . "99 Lives."

On your commute to work in your four-wheel drive, do you ever fantasize about moving to the mountains or seashore and working out of your own home so that you can get away from it all and spend more time with the kids? *Click* . . . "Cashing Out."

Have you bought a new book on the soul recently to help you reconnect with your lost self, your spiritual side, or have you started taking daily meditation breaks, or reinstituted family prayer and a home altar? *Click* . . . "Anchoring."

Popcorn says this last act foreshadows "the start of a Great Awakening," one of the greatest times of spiritual upheaval and religious revival" this country has ever seen.

And so it goes as sixteen postmodern trends are outlined. Popcorn has some interesting, entertaining, and sometimes important things to say about virtually everything. The style of *Clicking* is congruent with its subject: it gives away content and invites its readers to become futurists while instructing them in how to do it. It is interactive, with phone/fax/E-mail instead of footnotes.

Yet while Popcorn talks about increased tombstone rubbings, she ought to be discussing the gravestones of the future—which will be both above ground and on-line. If funeral directors understood what business they were really in, they would be offering sites in what I would call "Web Heaven," where angels would direct you to your very own interactive Web page so that your grandchildren can hear your favorite hymns, listen to you read your favorite verses of Scripture, watch video clips of your life, learn about your values, and jot down reminiscences of your life which can be shared by friends around the world.

After putting down this hefty volume and thinking about the readiness of the church (and me personally) for this postmodern future, I couldn't help but think of what Kevin Greene, the Pittsburgh linebacker, said once after the Steelers started the season 3-4: "Time for a gut check."

That's the way I feel about the third millennium of the church's history—time for a gut check. I have no doubt God will be in the future, but I worry deeply about whether my own tribe will be there. The church *can* lead the move into the new intellectual and technological territory of the now Information Age, soon-to-be Genetic Age. We are not condemned to endlessly rework the ideas of the thinkers of the old world. But first we must choose hope over despair. Ancient/future faith and hope.

There's a craving in this world to cling to the traditions of antiquity while at the same time technology catapults us forward. Ancient/future faith and hope do that.

> Hope is a response to the future, which has its foundations in the promises of God. It looks at the future as time for the completion of God's promise. But hope is not a doctrine about the future: it is a grace cultivated in the present, it is a stance in the present which deals with the future. As such it is misunderstood if it is valued only for the comfort it brings, as if it should say, "Everything is going to be all right in the future because God is in control of it. Therefore relax and be comforted." Hope operates differently. Christian hope alerts us to the possibilities of the future as a field of action, and as a consequence, fills the present with energy.
>
> —EUGENE PETERSON

"Never forget that only dead fish swim with the tide." This famous Malcolm Muggeridge motto is a favorite among those who deride the church's attempt to speak to the culture in ways that take into account trends and popular culture. The backlash is growing against "catching the waves" and riding them for the gospel. An authentic witness, the swelling crowd of cultural reactionaries argue, is always against the current. The church is called to swim against the stream without drowning, with all making waves.

Another opinion is expressed by Marshall McLuhan, called by some the "Aquinas of the Electronic Age." McLuhan liked to remind critics who chastised him for "trendinitis" that their refusal to deal with cultural trends would only guarantee those trends longer life and faster speed, as well as endanger one's own continued existence. McLuhan's own motto shifts the metaphor to a superhighway: "On a moving highway, the vehicle that backs up is accelerating in relation to the highway situation."

McLuhan's motto, rightly understood, does not minimize the church's role as the great dissenter of every age. At times, the church must be determined to go its own way; at times, the church will be criticized for being foolish, wrong, out-of-date, out-of-it, etc. Indeed, it is precisely to preserve dissidence as an essential quality of the Christian that the church must move not against the tide, not with the tide, but ahead of the tide. If the church is to demythologize the culture's myths instead of the culture always demythologizing the church; if the church is to critique the reigning myths of technism, scientism, miraculism, and their approach to life; if technologies are to be deflected so that they do not degenerate into unspeakable evil, then the church must be prepared to anticipate change and get ahead of the culture, not always be in a reactive—whether catch up or put down—posture. It's time for the church to invent the future.

Oh Israel, put your hope in the LORD both now and forevermore.
—PSALM 131:3 NIV

As the writer of Hebrews says, "We have this hope as an anchor for the soul, firm and secure. It enters the inner sanctuary behind the curtain, where Jesus, who went before us, has entered on our behalf" (Heb. 6:19 NIV). The Hebrews author goes on to say that faith is "the substance of things hoped for, the evidence of things not seen" (11:1 NKJV). Our foundation for living in the third millennium rests on this—we have faith for the future because we have hope in God's promises.

When I was in high school, I earned money during the summer by lifeguarding at various Christian camps in the Adirondack Mountains. One summer I worked at Sacandaga Bible Conference in Broadalbin, New York. Included in my job description was the task of taking teenagers on speedboat rides every afternoon. It was a tough assignment, but somebody had to do it! I quickly learned that there are two kinds of teenagers who go to Christian

camps. There are those who, when the engine is revved up and the throttle
let out, stand in the middle of the boat straddling the bounce across the
waves while yelling, "Faster, faster!" These are the wave-riders, and you can
see the exhilaration and excitement in their faces. Then there are a whole
other crew of campers who are not at the center of the boat, but are leaning
over the sides of the boat, clinging for dear life, hoping and praying that this
wonderful experience will soon be over. These are the boat-huggers. You can
tell this type from the looks of fear and panic on their faces, as well as from
some other physiological symptoms best described no further. Boat-huggers
and wave-riders: two very different types of mission for the church.

God calls the church to "aqua-esce" in God's mission—to leave the harbor, lift anchor, and launch out into the joy and risk of the deep sea. Our
mission is not to hug harbors, or drop anchors where it is safe, or cheer as
other boats sail into the deep. The place for the church is on the high seas
where it is turbulent and dangerous, where storms gather with their fiercest
intensity. In early Christian art, the church was portrayed as a boat driven
upon a perilous sea.

Jesus made this very clear to his disciples in Mark's account of Jesus
rebuking the storm. One evening an exhausted Jesus was sleeping on the little seat placed at the stern of Peter's boat when a sudden squall arose on the
notoriously stormy Sea of Galilee. As the splashing waves broke upon the
boat and the disciples found themselves bailing water, they panicked and
rushed to the stern of the boat where Jesus was sleeping. Shaking him vio-
lently, they cried out despairingly, "Master, the tempest is raging. The billows
are blasting high. Don't you care we are sinking?" Brushing off sleep, Jesus
arose, went briskly to the side of the boat, stretched out his arm, and spoke
peace to the storm: "Peace, be still" (Mark 4:35–41).

What a magic moment! What a privilege to have witnessed one of the
most spectacular miracles of Jesus' ministry, his subduing the waves and wind
with the mere sound of his voice. What a thrill to have been there for such
an event. But then immediately Jesus turned to his disciples angrily and
rebuked them: "Where is your faith!" They had missed the real blessing.
What could have been more of a thrill than witnessing this miracle of Jesus

calming the storm? The miracle Jesus wanted to show them was not the miracle of calming the storm, but of calming them in the storm.

Think what it would have been like to have experienced the miracle of wave-riding, the joy of knowing that no matter how fierce the storm, no matter how many crises in your cruises, nothing of ultimate harm could happen to you as long as you were in the boat with Jesus. With Jesus in our midst, there is nothing to fear!

But Jesus never promised to speak peace to every storm in our lives. In fact, Jesus' dictum to his disciples in Mark 13 was basically "in the world you shall have tribulation." But Jesus did promise to speak peace to us in the midst of every storm. One of the most beautiful prayers ever written is the traditional prayer of the Breton fisherman: O God, thy sea is so great and my boat is so small." Jesus is calling the church to be a community of wave-riders—people who will lift anchor from whatever holds them in life's harbors; people who will sail off into the high seas of ministry and mission; people who will believe that even when God does not calm the storms, God will calm them in the storms; people who will know that to voyage with Jesus is to enjoy peace even in storm-tossed experiences. The storms came upon the house built on the rock no differently than the house built on the sand. But it stood. The point is not to avoid storms, but to stand through the storms with Christ.

As John Wesley was making his way to Georgia from England aboard the merchant ship *Simmonds* in 1735, he watched in total amazement as a community of Moravian passengers continued to worship God and sing in the midst of an Atlantic storm as if nothing were happening. Wesley marveled at this kind of faith. Then he asked God to help him develop a faith for when the big storms blow. If more people were to see that kind of faith today, there would surely be a population explosion of wave-riding believers.

> I shall not truly live until I see God;
> when I have seen God, I shall never die.
>
> —MABEL BOGGS SWEET

Cecil B. DeMille, the one who first dramatically depicted biblical stories on the screen, was allegedly a person of devout faith. An active member of Christ's Episcopal Church of Pompton, New Jersey, DeMille was so sensitive in his movie portrayals to Christians that he sent an advance script of *The Ten Commandments* to religious leaders, including Southern Baptist pastor W. A. Criswell, for his review and critique. He displayed similar sensitivity in his other movies, *The King of Kings* and *The Sign of the Cross*.

Shortly before his death, DeMille wrote the following:

> One day as I was lying in a canoe, a big black beetle came out of the water and climbed up into the canoe. I watched it idly for some time. Under the heat of the sun, the beetle proceeded to die. Then a strange thing happened. His glistening black shell cracked all the way down his back. Out of it came a shapeless mass, quickly transformed into beautiful, brilliantly colored life.
>
> As I watched in fascination, there gradually unfolded iridescent wings from which the sunlight flashed a thousand colors. The wings spread wide, as if in worship of the sun. The blue-green body took shape. Before my eyes had occurred a metamorphosis—the transformation of a hideous beetle into a gorgeous dragonfly, which started dipping and soaring over the water. But the body it had left behind still clung to my canoe. I had witnessed what seemed to be a miracle. Out of the muck had come a beautiful new life. And the thought came to me, that if the Creator works such wonders with the lowliest of creatures, what may not be in store for the human spirit?

Great historical events might never have "happened" if people's spirits were not in touch with the Creator's movement in their lives:

The world's a better place because Michelangelo didn't say, "I don't do ceilings."

The world's a better place because a German monk named Martin Luther didn't say, "I don't do doors."

The world's a better place because an Oxford don named John Wesley didn't say, "I don't do fields."

The world's a better place because Moses didn't say, "I don't do Pharaohs."

The world's a better place because Noah didn't say, "I don't do arks and animals."

The world's a better place because Ruth didn't say, "I don't do mothers-in-law."

The world's a better place because Mary didn't say, "I don't do virgin births."

The world's a better place because Mary Magdalene didn't say, "I don't do feet."

The world's a better place because Jesus didn't say, "I don't do crosses."

Get in touch with the greatness of your physical and spiritual heritage. Look to the future, and feel God's Spirit stirring your own. Then watch in wonder as God transforms your life.

Chapter 9
GROWING A SOUL

There is no "The End" to be written, neither can you, like an architect, engrave in stone the day the garden was finished; a painter can frame his picture, a composer notate his coda, but a garden is always on the move. . . . This thing once started will never be quiescent; at no moment, however peerless, will a garden be immobile, petrified on this summit of flowering.

—MIRABEL OSLER

I had a gardener for a grandmother. Or as Gramma Boggs used to put it, she was a "dirt gardener," which printer/gardener Hal W. Trovillion defines as someone who mixes "soul with soil and seed." Gramma became a gardener because Grandad didn't like to farm. Mother used to say that if it weren't for Gramma, Grandad would have starved. Gramma took care of the fifty-two acres of farm in Brown Hollow (most of the land being mountain land).

Gramma had a sense of the land such that if you didn't have land, she believed, you had nothing. We were taught that it was more important for parents to leave land to their children than to leave money. One needed land for life. When you lose your land, you lose your life. Farmers can sell the land, put the proceeds into a 5.5 percent savings account, and make more money. But then they won't have any land. When I first realized this, I was scandalized. Think of all those poor farmers' kids spending all those twelve- to sixteen-hour, hot summer days working the farm when they could have worked a hammock and made more money. These people didn't own the land, I thought, the land owned them.

Exactly. That is why gardening is not just a vocation reserved for those who work with dirt. It is not only gardeners who should celebrate the first Earth Day—August 30, the feast day of St. Flacre de Breuil, the sixth-century patron saint of gardeners. For gardening is a universal vocation. Why gardening?

God calls us all to be earth-keepers or gardeners. That is the "first commandment" spelled out in Genesis, to tend and till the soil. In the Garden of Eden we lived in perfect harmony with God, and the earth was our first sacrament. Perhaps that is why we feel most in harmony with God when we are gardening. Or in the words of Phyllis Theroux, "I think this is what hooks one on gardening; it is the closest one can come to being present at the Creation." The pilgrimage of life is the way back to that first Garden—a pilgrimage that takes us through some other gardens, like the Garden of Gethsemane and the Garden of the Tomb. Even so, "there can be no other occupation like gardening in which, if you were to creep up behind someone at their work, you would find them smiling," Theroux concludes.

What do gardeners do? They grow things. Teachers are gardeners—they grow curious and creative minds. Pastors are gardeners—they grow souls, they grow communities of faith. Philosophers are gardeners—they grow beauty, truth, and goodness. Politicians are gardeners—they grow justice, peace, and security. Physicians are gardeners—they grow healthy bodies.

Gardeners are people who grow things. Whatever we do, we garden. When you sit at your word processor, you are gardening with words and phrases. When you sit at the piano, you are gardening with notes and silences. When you stand at the stove, you are gardening with meats, vegetables, sugars, and spices. When you lie in bed with your spouse, you are gardening with glands, genes, and grace. When you gather in a circle and brainstorm, you are gardening with your dreams and desires.

There is an old French saying: "Chase away nature and it comes back at a gallop." Mountain pieties are a form of earth wisdom that we ignore at our own peril. There are five principles of good gardening my mountain Gramma taught me. They are principles of growing a soul which we chase away at the cost of a boomeranging stampede. They are:

1. Don't get rid of your seed corn.

2. There's no use watering last year's crops.

3. Feed the soil and the soil will feed you in return.

4. Rain is not something you should always come out of.

5. God doesn't settle all accounts in October.

Follow these five life principles of gardening and I predict you will say with Mary of old, as she ran from the Garden early that first Easter morning, "I have seen the Lord!"

DON'T GET RID OF YOUR SEED CORN

There were corollaries to this saying, like, "You can't harvest what you don't sow," or "You can't sow where you're afraid to plant," or "If you don't turn over the soil enough, you get weeds" . . . or half-plowed people. But the seed corn metaphor was as important to my mountain Gramma then as it is to software guru Bill Gates today.

The sowing of seed is one of the most fundamental of all gardening activities. Humans don't live without sowing seed, which accounts for the motto of the American Seed Trade Association: "First—the Seed." Seed is the basis of crop growing, and a little seed sown goes a long way in growing a big crop.

One day inventor/statesman Benjamin Franklin observed a broom corn seed in a whisk broom. A broom corn seed is one of the millets—it belongs in the grass family. Franklin planted it, and from that one seed grew up the booming broom corn industry in America. One little seed created an entire industry.

Gramma raised tomatoes, beans, sugar cane, and corn in the days before "Easter Egg" radishes and "Red Sails" lettuce and "Sugar Snap" peas. In other words, Gramma gardened in the days before the commodification of the seed, as found in seed packets and seed catalogues. Seed has now become big business, so much so that farmers are legally restrained from keeping the seed of certain proprietary varieties for the resowing of next year's crops. Some of the hottest ethical issues in the future will be brought to us by biotechnology's ability to tamper with seeds.

Jesus told a parable about the seed once, which reads:

And [Jesus] said, "The kingdom of God is as if a man should scatter seed on the ground, and should sleep by night and rise by day, and the seed should sprout and grow, he himself does not know how. For the earth yields crops by itself: first the blade, then the head, after that the full grain in the head. But when the grain ripens, immediately he puts in the sickle, because the harvest has come." Then he said, "To what shall we liken the kingdom of God? Or with what parable shall we picture it? It is like a mustard seed which, when it is sown on the ground, is smaller than all the seeds on earth; but when it is sown, it grows up and becomes greater than all herbs, and shoots out large branches so that the birds of the air may nest under its shade." And with many such parables He spoke the word to them as they were able to hear it. But without a parable He did not speak to them. And when they were alone, He explained all things to His disciples.

—MARK 4:26–34 NKJV

My Gramma had her own unique commentary on this verse. She would take a seed in her hand and push it into the faces of me and my brothers. Then she would shake the seed and announce that when we go to college, our science professors there will tell us precisely what seeds are made of. They know the exact proportion of nitrogen, hydrogen, and carbon. Gramma also predicted that by then scientists would be able to make seeds out of these precise ingredients that would look exactly like the one in her hand.

Then Gramma would raise herself up proudly and conclude her lecture: "Do you boys know what will happen when they plant that seed, water it, weed it, watch it? Nothing, that's what. No crop will ever come of it. Why? It is missing the God force.

"Never get rid of your seed corn" was my Gramma's way of reminding me never to take for granted, never to leave behind or put aside, those things that made me who I am—my family, friends, and faith.

What is our seed corn as Christians? Our seed corn is the Word and words of God. The Word (capital W) of God is Christ. The words (small w) of God are the Scriptures. The Bible is not the Word of God, but the words of God; or as Luther phrased the relationship between the Word and the words, "The Scriptures are the manger in which Christ is laid."

"You can't keep eating the big potatoes and still have them." H. L. Lucenay calls this the "Law of Small Potatoes," based on the ancient story of Chinese farmers who decided they would eat the good big potatoes and use the small ones for seed. The more they kept up this practice, keeping for themselves the biggest and saving the smallest, the leftovers, for seed, the more Nature reduced all their potatoes to the size of marbles.

The harvest reflects the planting. Selfishness is not rewarded with blessings. Plant small potatoes and you will get small potatoes.

Christ is our seed corn. In the words of 1 Corinthians 3:22–23: "The world, life, death, the present, the future, are all yours. But you are Christ's, and Christ is God's" (author's translation). The Scriptures point us to the Christ; they show us what happens when the seed corn of faith in Christ is planted and what harvests we can expect.

My Gramma did not keep the Bible cooped up in some "parson's cupboard" alongside the fireplace, to be frantically brought out and dusted off when the preacher came calling. She was one of those self-educated readers (she only went through the fourth grade) who "meditated day and night" (Ps. 1:2) on particular passages, whose pages in her Bible were so well broken in that the Wesleyan Methodist preacher who officiated at her funeral picked the Scriptures to be read simply by letting her Bible plop itself open to her favorite verses.

How many of these verses Gramma knew by heart, or read, we will never know for sure. But when I first read the following story in Princeton historian Albert Raboteau's masterful study of "slave religion," I could not help but think of my Gramma.

One freedman who visited a night school for emancipated slaves in Beaufort, North Carolina, tells the story of a black woman who carried a big Bible with her through the swamps and the woods. Though she was unable to read, she "had got her old mistress to turn down the leaves at the verses she knew by heart, and often she would sit down in the woods and open the big Bible at these verses, and repeat them aloud, and find strength and consolation."

Gramma taught her grandchildren that we must never take for granted that we hold in our hand, and place on our nightstands, the single most important book in the history of the planet. Every one of us can grasp in the palm of our hands the greatest story ever told—yea, the book our family believed "to be true, whatever is recorded in the Word, for the authority of God speaketh therein"—words my Presbyterian-minister-brother John memorized long ago from the Westminster Confession.

Gramma loved to tell Civil War stories about soldiers who took their Bibles into battle with them, Bibles their mamas and grammas had given them, and were saved both spiritually and physically when a bullet hit their bodies but did not penetrate the skin, slowed by the Bible resting on their chest. I loved the stories, but always wanted to see one of those bullet-nabbing Bibles. The closest I have ever come was in California, where a pastor showed me a small, handsome Bible printed in 1859 with the inscription:

> Mr. Loer M. Soper
> Presented to him by
> his mother
> on the 10th day of
> September, 1861
> Loer M. Soper

In the back of the book, in beautiful penmanship, it reads: "This book was presented by mother on the morning of September 10, 1861, with her earnest request that I should make myself familiar with its contents. That morning I left my home and all that was dear to me in this world to join my company and Regt. at Ogendsburgh, New York. I have since passed through many scenes of trial and danger and have had some experience in battling with life but 'this book,' its great truths, together with Mother's last words, have thus far preserved me, by God's goodness and mercy. Washington D.C., January 20th, 1867, L. M. Soper."

The verses well marked in this Bible, verses that helped Loer Soper get through many Civil War battles as well as "battling with life," included Romans 8:10–11; 2 Corinthians 5:1–4; Galatians 5:16; James 5:7; and 1 Peter 5:8. Especially worn were the Psalms. The more I think about it, I can say with conviction that I have once held in my hand, if ever there were one, a bullet-nabbing Bible.

> Give fools their gold and
> knaves their power,
> Let fortune's bubbles
> rise and fall,
> Who sows a field or trains
> a flower or plants a tree,
> is more than all.
>
> —JOHN GREENLEAF WHITTIER

One of the most unforgettable stories of the West is that of a young couple who went out to homestead more than a century ago. Out of the virgin forests of the wild West they molded a farm. They used supplies that nature gave them and built a cabin. Their children were born there. Every couple of months the father had to go to town to get supplies. The town was not close by; in fact, it was so far away that he had to stay overnight each trip.

One time the farmer had just left the cabin for town when his wife was walking through the tall grass outside and stepped on a deadly snake. Its fatal poison was injected into her system and, of course, no medical aid was available. What was she to do? Her husband wouldn't be returning for days! Her first thought was for her children. She ran inside, built a fire in the primitive stove, and began cooking everything she could get her hands on in order that the children would have food. The cabin became terribly hot and the perspiration seemed to be running from every pore in her body. As she worked feverishly, she explained to the children that she would be taking a long nap, but that when she got through cooking, there would be an ample supply for them to eat. She assigned chores to each child. The faster and harder she worked the sicker she became. Strength seemed to ooze from her sweating body, but she pushed herself as she had never done before in order to ensure adequate provisions for her children until their father returned. Not wanting to collapse onto the floor and frighten the kids, with her last strength she laid down and passed out. Her children watched helplessly as her body went through all the symptoms of snake-bite poisoning.

When the farmer returned, the children rushed to meet him. "Something's wrong! Mama's been asleep for days," they said. He found his wife still breathing, and terribly sick, but still alive. When the doctor was called and finally arrived, he examined her incredulously and asked what had happened. The farmer could only explain her survival by conjecturing that she had worked so hard because of her love for those children that she had literally sweat some of the poisons out of her system, saving her life.

The twenty-first century will be filled with untold toxins of the mind, toxins of the body, toxins of the spirit. The more I walk into the future, the more I understand why Gramma's favorite hymn was "Rock of Ages, Cleft for Me/Let Me Hide Myself in Thee." There is only one thing that will save us and bring us safely through. That is if our love for the Word of God and the words of the Scriptures make us work so hard for a dying world that we sweat every toxin, every poison, every hatred out of our system.

 History proves that it has never been possible to destroy a faith grounded in Scripture, even with the most devastating revolutions in the state.

—IMMANUEL KANT

Lest Gramma's first principle of good gardening be mistaken, here's one more reflection. Preserving one's seed corn does not mean hoarding it and not sharing it with others. Theologian John M. Drescher tells the story about the corn farmer who won all the blue ribbons for his corn year after year at the surrounding fairs. Yet each year he shared his best seed corn with all his neighbors.

"How do you expect to continue to win blue ribbons," someone asked him, "if you give your best seed corn to others?"

"You don't understand," said the farmer. "The wind carries the pollen from field to field. If I am to have the best corn, I must see to it that all my neighbors also have the best corn. If they produce poor corn it will pollinate mine and pull my quality down."

So it is with all of life. We are all gardening the same plot of ground. The quality of our life has a direct bearing on the quality of our neighbor's life.

THERE'S NO USE WATERING LAST YEAR'S CROPS

Actually, these are not my Gramma's words. But they are the way I remember my Gramma's words. "There's no use watering last year's crops" comes from a line from writer/translator George Eliot: "It's but little good you'll do watering last year's crops." My Gramma's way of putting it was vintage Appalachian: "There's no use crying over spilt milk." By this she meant worrying about things that can't be changed; fretting over things done that should not have been done, and things that should have been done but weren't; being fixated on your failures, unable to forget and go on with life.

Two people are talking. One says, "My friend has a terrible memory, the worst memory I ever heard of." The other responds, "Forgets everything, huh?" "No!" the first responds. "Remembers everything!"

Paul talks of how in his own life he had to forget those things that were past: "Forgetting what lies behind . . . I press on" (Phil. 3:13–14). The opening lines of Aldous Huxley's novel *Brave New World* offer an alternative translation of Paul's reminder to forget: "Rolling in the muck is not the best way of getting clean."

"You boys are just growing like a weed," Gramma used to say after she hadn't seen us for a while. But when she got frustrated with our mischief and couldn't take our messiness anymore, she'd look down, and then look up and say, "I'm just gonna cut my suspenders and go straight up!" Gramma had high expectations of all her grandchildren. One of her litanies of life—"Do it right or don't do it at all"—came like this in the poetic format: "If a task is once begun/Never leave it till its done/Be it great or be it small, Do it right or don't do it at all." But she also knew that whatever we did, even when it was most right, would also have some wrong in it. Gramma knew that everyone's grasp exceeded their gain, or in words I have grown to cherish, "Starting a garden is the beginning of making a series of mistakes." That's why it's so comforting that there are stories about weeds in the Bible (Matt. 13:24–30). We all have to live life among the weeds. There are no perfect fields. Every crop of wheat must learn to live with the weeds.

From a child's viewpoint, it seemed at times as if Gramma relished cultivating the weeds herself. "How long until supper?" we would ask. Gramma sometimes would reply impishly, "Three shakes of a dead sheep's tail!" "What are we going to have for supper?" we'd ask further. "Pig's ass and cabbage" (that's ham and cabbage for you city folks). Then she would laugh to herself, knowing that we were scandalized. Gramma, who wouldn't even let us use slang, had just sworn and we didn't know what to do about it!

But learning to live with and among the weeds is not the same thing as substituting them for crop. When one lives off a crop of weeds, when one constantly waters last year's crop, one becomes the kind of Christian my Grandad Boggs used to complain about. Some church members were like one farmer's pond, he said, "dried up in the summer and frozen over in the winter."

Katherine Hepburn's autobiography, titled *Me: Stories of My Life,* captures the difference between living with and living off weeds nicely.

And I was thinking. You have now discovered the truth about yourself. Your parents gave you a great start. You were planted in good soil—fed, watered, carefully nurtured. And you were sent out into the world. And you were lucky. And apparently you have been successful. But have you accomplished all that you could have, given your beginning? No, you have been careless, you did not get to the essence of things. You can't do this and you can't do that, and you could have if you had concentrated and just stuck to it and got to the bottom of it. It's a bit late now, but profit by this—if you do it, do it. Get those weeds out. And plant carefully.

The power of even a lone worry, a single fret, a solitary weed to stop life in its tracks and keep the soul from growing, is brought home to me every time an airplane lands. As I uncurl my lanky frame from the window seat, I watch out the porthole in amazement as a solitary figure saunters to the plane and places a small block of wood in front of its wheels. Here is one of the most powerful machines ever invented, outfitted with the most sophisticated technology in the world, and it is effectively blocked from going anywhere by a little piece of wood that would be too small for many of our fireplaces.

It doesn't take much to prevent us from going anywhere, or to cause us to "climb up the rough side of the mountain" (as the song goes). One failure that we keep wedging in our wheels, one mistake that we keep dragging with us, one foul-up that we won't bury and forget—that's all it takes to bring life to a grinding halt, and to prevent the soul from taking off.

A woman dreamed she walked into a brand new shop in a brand new mall. She was more than a little surprised to discover Jesus behind the counter. "What kind of merchandise is for sale here?" the woman asked. "Everything to fulfill all your burning desires," Jesus answered. The woman couldn't believe her ears: everything to fulfill all her burning desires?

After thinking it over, she decided to ask for only the very best things that any human being could passionately desire. "I would like to have peace of mind, and love, and freedom from fear, and genuine happiness," she finally said, then added, "And not just for me, but for the whole world . . . for everyone on the face of the earth."

Jesus smiled. "Perhaps you are misunderstanding," he said. "We don't sell fruits here. We only sell seeds."

FEED THE SOIL AND THE SOIL WILL FEED YOU IN RETURN

Gramma used to say this in conjunction with another admonition to Grandad before he went out to work in the sawmill: "Plant a tree everywhere you cut one down." She would repeat this over and over, much to Grandad's annoyance.

The first requirement of a good gardener is: Know the seasons. A garden is never the same two years running; the seasons are always changing. Know your garden well enough that you can sense when to work the garden and when to rest the garden. This has become one of the rules of organic gardening. Life needs fallow fields, green spaces, and empty places. We all need a break from the business of making an effort.

Gramma was insistent that her progeny turn every Sunday into a Sabbath. Her way of putting this need to "hallow" some time in our lives was "Now's Sabbath time." Substitute the word "soul" for "soil" in this principle, and it helps to explain Gramma's strictness about the Sabbath. Sabbathness enables us to have the energy to work creatively and faithfully. Ursula K. LeGuin says: "If you haven't got something to put it in, food will escape you."

Gramma liked to work hard. When people said to her, "You work so hard!" she would say in return, "I'm going to take my vacation in heaven." But Gramma also knew the principle of "Sabbath time." Brought up a Baptist, Gramma was rigid about her Lord's Day. My aunts and uncles and we grandkids couldn't even file a fingernail on Sunday. There was no ball playing, no hide-and-seek, no running wildly through the house. We had to stay dressed up in our Sunday best all day. It seemed as though all we could do on Sunday was go to church, sing hymns, or take a walk. A Sunday schedule at Gramma's went something like this: It began like every other day, with a tradition of early rising. At 7 A.M. the family gathered around the big table, with everyone dressed in their best clothes. Whenever the Boggs clan gathered together, Grandad asked the Lord's blessing (Gramma could read the Scriptures, but she never prayed at table). At the sound of the "Amen," everyone delved into a feast of bacon, eggs, hot biscuits, oatmeal, or, on special days, mush or hominy grits—a breakfast treat Gramma cooked on that giant woodstove she loved and refused to abandon. No one got up from the table until Grandad led everyone in family prayer. Then the chairs were pushed back and everyone knelt at the table for a time of Bible reading and more prayer.

While the table was being cleaned, the rest of us put on the finishing touches for church. It was then off to Sunday school (where Grandad was the superintendent), followed by church. Sunday dinner was the biggest meal of the week, both in terms of food on, and people at, the table. I knew firsthand the expression "like a chicken with its head cut off," for Gramma always made enough food for extra guests—*fresh* southern fried chicken, gravy, pinto beans, and "greens" (spring poke greens with onions were my favorite) cooked in fatback, bread, sliced tomatoes, coleslaw, and pickles. Even if there were no visiting preachers or musicians to join us for Sunday dinner, a place at the table was left open as a symbol of our family's hospitality to strangers.

Sunday afternoons hardly ever seemed to me like lost causes, as novelist Tom Robbins remembered them—things "carved . . . from a boiled turnip." Far from lonely, boring, depressing times, Sunday afternoon was the primary time for visiting relatives and friends in neighboring hollers, or when weather didn't permit ("Lord willin' and the creek don't rise," Gramma always used to preface her intentions), playing the pump organ and singing hymns around the piano. On special occasions Gramma got out her dulcimer or banjo. Even more special were the times she and Grandad sang a duet, his bass voice blending beautifully with her soprano lead. There was also a Boggs family tradition of helping out small country churches by leading worship and singing at 3 P.M. services. Sunday supper was always early and light: mush and milk or pinto beans and corn bread dipped into buttermilk. Sunday evening services were never an option, always an obligation.

When I was growing up I protested the strictness of these Sunday regulations. Today they stand as some of the most pleasant memories of my life. Carlo Caretto says to "make some desert in your life." We all need to set aside desert days, fallow fields that are not being constantly plowed up with our own agendas and ambitions.

The Jewish tradition has done better than Christians have in understanding this injunction. The great nineteenth-century Jewish philosopher Samson Raphael Hirsch insisted that the Sabbath serve to remind us of who is master of creation, and to whom creation belongs. "Humanity is allowed to rule over the earth for six days with God's will and approval. On the seventh day, however, humanity is forbidden . . . to fashion anything for our own purpose." The Sabbath is God's day, the day on which everything goes back to God for God to set right again.

Psalm 23 says God "maketh me lie down in green pastures." Sometimes God makes us slow down and let our fields go fallow. Sometimes we are forced to take vacations through illness. Proust used to argue that "disease is the best doctor—it forces the patient to cure himself." Or as the graffiti philosopher has written: "Death can be nature's way of saying to the body: 'Slow down!'" John Stroman puts it more gently: "A life out-of-balance is like a tire out-of-balance on your car; both wear out quickly." Green pastures, still waters, and soul restoration go together. A life overbrimming and running over with plans, appointments, and anxieties is not a healthy life. Without rest, the heavy-laden lifestyle (Matt. 11:28) leads to mental and spiritual infertility.

Psalm 46:10 reads, "Pause a while and know that I am God," or in the New English translation, "Let be then: learn that I am God." Might this be the reason why God spent so much time explaining what is meant by the Fourth Commandment—Remember the Sabbath Day, to keep it holy— than any other commandment?

Mozart was fond of saying, "I can tell a good musician by the way he plays the rests." Christians can't afford to ignore the "rests" and the "silences," for they are the very things that make us good musicians. You have to lounge to live; you have to be recreated to receive fresh messages from God. By recreation I do not mean amusement parks and bowling alleys, although these may be recreational. Recreation means re-creation— what supplies your soulbody with the energy you need to be creative. Recreation literally re-creates your soul.

 I loaf and invite my Soul, I lean and loaf at my ease,
            observing a spear of summer grass.
                    —WALT WHITMAN

RAIN IS NOT SOMETHING YOU SHOULD ALWAYS COME OUT OF

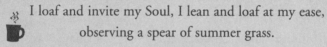

Actually, this is something Gramma Boggs said to my mother, not to my brothers and me. Back in the days when children still had fields and streams and creeks in which to play, my brothers and I liked to go out and wade in Waid's Creek (pronounced "crik"; in West Virginia we take out the "worsh," not the "wash") when it rained. The creek came alive in the rain like it never did in the sunshine.

But the mother gene has this thing about children playing in the rain. My mother was forever calling us to "get out of the rain," sometimes following it up with the exhortation to "get in the house and take your Saturday night bath." One time, Gramma had taken about as much of this as she could. Maybe she didn't inherit that anti-rain mother gene; at any rate, where normally she didn't interfere with mother's childrearing practices, this time she defended us vigorously, saying to her daughter, "Mabel, rain is not something the boys always have to come out of."

Part of growing up is, by definition, knowing when to come in out of the rain. Anthropologist Clifford Geertz divides "common sense opinion" into two parts: the knowledge that rain makes us wet, and the sense that wetness is unwelcome. The older we get, the more mature we become, the more the second part of that common sense equation gets set in concrete. Childish behavior scorns the elements. Good and proper adultish behavior takes shelter. The rain bothers us. Indeed, in our adultish ways of thinking, rain is a hurting symbol of everything that goes wrong. Into everyone's life, so it is said, some rain (interpreted 'hurt') must fall.

> Rain messes us up.
> Rain ruins our respectability.
> Rain makes our hair look bad.
> The mixture of rain and hair spray is a wild look.
> Drunk on respectability,
> we come not to like "singing in the rain."
> Besides, the terminal velocity of a raindrop is 22 mph.

And doesn't it always seem that when it rains, it pours? In the wonderful words of Jules Renard: "There are moments when everything turns out right. Don't let it alarm you—they pass." No one likes the rain. Indeed, rain has even been made a curse, as in the Burch Sisters' country song, "Every Time You Go Outside I Hope It Rains."

Life is an unequal and unpredictable mixture of sunshine and rain. Without moisture, blossoms don't bloom. No rain, no growth. All sunshine turns life into a desert. And when we always come out of the rain, fail to let the rain drain into our being—the very waters of life—our lives fail to bear fruit. There's also something therapeutic for adults who can relearn how to play in the rain. If you can let go of all the inhibitions that pile up with respectability (like the bad hair), playing in the rain can be kind of cathartic, like recreating childhood. Good gardeners know what grows best in sunlight and what grows best in shade or rain, just as God knows best which of us needs to be planted in the sunshine, and which of us needs to be nestled in a shady nook or rain-soaked bit of earth.

Disciples of Jesus Christ must learn to stand the rain if the gospel is going to get outdoors where the people are. Churches where Jesus Christ lives don't stay indoors, in comfort zones, protected from the storms of our world and the rough places of our journey. Indeed, communities of faith must be willing to enter the danger zones, the unsafe, unproven, out-of-control places where the social lepers and outsiders and voiceless live. Gramma unwittingly taught me to break out of control and comfort to chance life with God.

One more word about life's rhythm of sunshine and rain. It comes from author Alice Caldwell Rice: "Ain't no use putting up your umbrella till it rains." Too many people are going around with umbrellas unfurled, living as if it were raining in the midst of life's most wondrously glorious days.

There are certain strategies one can adopt that will get you through a downpour in as dry a state as possible if you're forced to walk through the rain. I didn't learn this from Gramma; I learned this from science.

There is a scientific method for getting through the rain that has deep soul implications. First, *keep moving.* In fact, run as fast as you can. The faster you go, the fewer the raindrops that hit you. A physicist in the European *Journal of Physics* asked the question, "Is it really worth running in the rain?" and found out that the worst thing you can do in a storm is to stop. When the rains hit, don't let them slow you down. In fact, pick up your speed.

Second, *lean forward in the direction you want to go.* Rain is no time for indecision, vacillation, or soul searching. Save those activities for sunny days. When it rains, lean as far as you can in the direction you're going. The farther you lean forward, the less wet you get. The number of drops hitting you from above won't change, but the number of drops hitting you in the face from the front will drop as you diminish your surface area exposed to the rain.

Third, *be flexible enough to make adjustments on the run depending on which way the wind is blowing.* If the storm is coming at you from the front or even the side, there is no need to change direction. But if the storm comes at you from behind and hits you in the back rather than the face, be prepared to make some adjustments. Otherwise you'll get four times wetter than you need to because you'll be catching up to and smashing into raindrops.

Finally, there is one rain storm in which, at least theoretically, you can stay absolutely dry. It's the worst rainstorm imaginable—worse than a hurricane, a tornado, a monsoon—a rainstorm that blows so hard and fast the water moves parallel with the ground. If by some superhuman feat you could match your speed to the horizontal speed of the rain, you'd stay perfectly dry. As my friend and teacher Jay Ingram puts it, "You'd never catch up to the drops ahead of you, the drops behind couldn't catch you, and nothing would fall on your head because they're all traveling horizontally."

This is precisely how I have come to understand the power of resurrection over death.

GOD DOESN'T SETTLE ALL ACCOUNTS IN OCTOBER

My Gramma sympathized with dairy farmers. "The hardest thing about milking cows is they never stay milked," she'd often say. But the point I remember her making the most was "not everybody who feeds the cow gets to drink the milk." We may not think that is fair, but that is life.

One of the biggest advertising myths today is the "people get what they deserve" line. The truth is, you don't always get what you deserve in life. Life is not always fair, and "bad things happen to good people." There are no guarantees. None of us (not the best or the worst of us) can be sure how things will turn out in life.

Ever get stopped for speeding when other cars have been passing you left and right? You feel like saying, "Officer, why didn't you ticket those people?" I heard about a man who did say that, to which the officer replied, "I would but I can't catch them." Jack Benny was once given an award. He accepted it with these words: "I don't deserve this award. On the other hand, I have arthritis and I don't deserve that either."

You don't get what you deserve in life. Disease, like snowfall and sunshine, falls on the just and unjust alike. Does anybody deserve to die of cancer? Does anyone deserve to die of AIDS? Does anybody ever get what they deserve in life, either way? In fact, essayist/novelist Leo Tolstoy based his work "The Death of Ivan Illych" on precisely this theme. It is the story of a good man who lives his whole life according to the highest standards of society in hopes of gaining status, acceptance, prosperity, and happiness. Instead of enjoying the rewards of his good behavior, however, Ivan Illych endures an agonizing death. In his suffering he cries out, in effect, "Then what does it mean? Why? It can't be that life is so senseless and horrible. There is something wrong! This shouldn't be happening to me. Maybe I did not live as I ought to have done. But how could that be, when I did everything so properly? How could a God of love and justice rule over such a messed-up world? God may be in the heavens, but all's not right with the world! It's the mean, not the meek, that seem to be inheriting the earth."

Gramma was especially sensitive to those who got riches unfairly. She used to say that some people had as many faces as buckwheat; every way you look at them, they have a different face. We knew exactly what she meant, since a buckwheat has three faces. It used to make her mad, but then she would say, quoting that Memphis Baptist preacher, Robert G. Lee, "Payday—Someday." Not that things balance out. Hear Psalm 44:23: "Wake up, O God, why are you asleep?" And Malachi 2:17: "Where is the God of justice?" (author's translation). Or Psalm 13, "How long, O LORD? Wilt thou forget me forever? How long wilt thou hide thy face from me? How long must I bear pain in my soul and have sorrow in my heart all the day? How long shall my enemy be exalted over me?" There are times when it seems the poet A. E. Housman was right when he said, "Malt does more than Milton can/To justify God's way to man."

My Gramma died my first year in college (March 22, 1966, three months after my grandparents celebrated their fiftieth wedding anniversary). She died without ever knowing what an impact she had on my life. She didn't get what she deserved from me. While she was alive I never appreciated how important she was in my life. Had my Gramma gotten what she deserved, she would be alive to read this.

Do you expect your children to thank you for being such outstanding parents? Do you expect to hear before you die, "Mom, Dad, you were the best parents anyone could ever have had?"

Hello?!

Not on your life! Or at least not in most of our lives. Did you get the parents you deserved when you were growing up? Or more precisely, did you get the parents you deserved while they were still alive? How many of us wish we had said something to our parents while they were still with us?

This is where patience comes in.

One definition of patience is "the calm abiding of the issue of time, the quality of expecting long without rage or discontent." Patience comes from the Latin word for "to suffer." A patient is one who suffers. We are all patients in life—we all suffer lack of appreciation, credit, glory, etc. It is these "undeserving" treatments that often teach us just how much patience and hope there really is in us.

The poet Henry Longfellow was devastated by the news that his beloved son had been wounded serving with the Army of the Potomac during the Civil War. He had been taken to the hospital, which most often meant death. Once a soldier entered the hospital, his problems really started. For example, American soldiers of the Revolutionary War had only a 2 percent chance of dying on the battlefield, but a 75 percent chance of perishing after treatment in the hospital. The real enemy once there—disease—was responsible for 90 percent of the deaths. In his pain and agony, Longfellow wrote a poem:

> I hear the bells on Christmas Day
> Their old familiar carols play. . . .
> And in despair I bowed my head,
> There is no peace on earth, I said.
> For hate is strong and mocks this song
> Of peace on earth, good will to men.
> Then pealed the bells more loud and deep,

> God is not dead, nor doth he sleep.
> The wrong shall fail, the right prevail,
> With peace on earth, good will to men.

But we already know how it all turns out! God is in charge of life, not evil. "That O the wrong seems oft so strong, God is the ruler yet," in the words of the Presbyterian hymn, "This is My Father's World."

This is not optimism; this is hope. Optimism, as the late historian Christopher Lasch put it in "True and Only Heaven," is a moral energy that is "insufficiently demanding." That is why our culture, immersed in selfish pursuits and private pleasures, is awash in optimism rather than hope. "Hope does not demand a belief in progress. It demands a belief in justice; a conviction that the wicked will suffer, that wrongs will be made right, that the underlying order of things is not flouted with impunity."

Hope is the belief that what little contributions and differences I make in my life have enduring and cumulative consequences. A friend of mine, Jaime Potter-Miller, told me a story once that took place when she served as a chaplain at the Asbury-Heights Retirement Community in Western Pennsylvania. She found herself making pastoral calls one afternoon on some of the there-but-not-there residents. How does one provide pastoral care to a woman in the later stages of Alzheimer's or to a *non compos mentis* man, she wondered?

Jaime determined that one way of caring for these people was to bring her guitar and sing. There was one patient in particular, however, for whom even singing seemed a waste of time. A brain stem stroke had left this woman virtually comatose, with not even a twitch of response to any stimuli in years. Her family had tried everything they could to reach her, but nothing evoked even a semblance of recognition.

Unable to bypass this woman's bed, Jaime bent down with her guitar as close to the woman's face as she could get, and began singing. "I wonder what she sang when she went to Sunday school?" Jaime asked herself. She sang her answers, one of which was "Great Is Thy Faithfulness." During this song, Jaime thought she heard a groaning sound. Then she watched in amazement as this stroke victim began to make guttural noises. She stopped singing, afraid that the woman was having another stroke, and called the nurse.

The nurse examined the woman and found her no different than usual. "You had to be imagining it," she said to Jaime. "This woman hasn't had any bodily response to anything or anyone in years." But Jaime wouldn't let her go.

"Listen to this," Jaime insisted. Once again she sang "Great Is Thy Faithfulness." And once again the woman began making those sighs and sounds "too deep for words."

The nurse bolted out of the room, collected every other medical staff person she could find, and brought them in to witness a miracle. A simple song had reached into this woman's soul and touched her where nothing else could. "Len," Jaime later said to me, "I had no idea how deep the roots of faith go down."

> If you wish to be happy for a week, have a big feast.
> If you wish to be happy for a year, get married.
> If you wish to be happy for life, plant a garden.
>
> —ANCIENT CHINESE PROVERB

Chapter 10
THE FRAGRANCE OF INTEGRITY

One time Jesus was wrong.

"Wherever the good news is proclaimed in the whole world, what she has done will be told in remembrance of her," the gospel reads. Yet in two thousand years, have we done what Jesus said we would do? Might it not be long overdue for us to do what Jesus said we *should* do, and make him right? Why did Jesus say what he did about this woman?

While he was at Bethany in the house of Simon the leper, as he sat at the table, a woman came with an alabaster jar of very costly ointment of nard, and she broke open the jar and poured the ointment on his head.

> But some were there who said to one another in anger,
> "Why was the ointment wasted in this way?
> For this ointment could have been sold for more than three hundred
> denarii, and the money given to the poor."
> And they scolded her.
> But Jesus said, "Let her alone; why do you trouble her?

She has performed a good service for me. For you always have the poor with you, and you can show kindness to them whenever you wish; but you will not always have me. "She has done what she could; she has anointed my body beforehand for its burial. Truly I tell you, wherever the good news is proclaimed in the whole world, what she has done will be told in remembrance of her."

—MARK 14:3–9 NRSV

In the Gospel of Mark, this act inaugurates the Triduum, which in Latin means "three days," or "The Great Three Days" or "Three Holy Days" of Maundy Thursday, Good Friday, and Holy Saturday, including the Easter Vigil. The Triduum is the holiest time of the Christian year.

In other words, this story inaugurates Mark's account of the last hours of Jesus' life. For Mark, Jesus' Passion begins with the story of the anointing woman and her deed of true love, devotion, and obedience to the Spirit, one of the last kindnesses Jesus received while on this earth.

> Oil and perfume make the heart glad.
> —PROVERBS 27:9

What is spikenard, some may ask. Spikenard, or nard, was the favorite perfume of antiquity. It got its name from the spike-like shape of the root and spiny stem of the herb plant which was found high up in the Himalayan mountains in India. The Greeks and Romans both loved the smell of this rare unguent so much that they willingly paid the expense of having it shipped long distances. The best spikenard was sealed in ornately-carved alabaster containers which were opened only on very special occasions. The magic of nard, and the pleasure of its perfume, is made clear in this simple verse from John 12: "And the house was filled with the fragrance of the ointment."

At the time of this story (told in three of the four Gospels), the cost of the perfume was three hundred denarii, or approximately a laborer's yearly wage. In today's terms, it would cost about thirty thousand dollars! If denarii were translated into pieces of silver, Jesus was betrayed and crucified for one-tenth the cost of this jar of perfume. In Jesus' circle, this kind of extravagance—a year's salary for one moment of luxury—was unheard of! This being the case, the disciples' reaction to the woman breaking the alabaster jar over Jesus' head was understandable.

Here was a woman who broke into the company of men, not carrying food from the kitchen—which was a woman's rightful place—but carrying the most expensive perfume of the ancient world.

Here was a woman who took it upon herself to break the flask and anoint Jesus during the meal, not before it.

Here was a woman who at that moment believed the person of Jesus was more important than any principle, even the principle of charity or helping the poor.

Here was a woman who believed Jesus when his disciples didn't. On three prior occasions, Jesus tried to warn his disciples that there would be trouble ahead, even suffering and death. Each time they dismissed his warnings, and proved so clueless that they got into a squabble over the power structure of the church (who is going to sit at Jesus' right and left hand?).

Here was a woman who got what Jesus was saying when he called us to live "incarnationally" in the midst of the pain and mire of poverty.

Here was a woman who knew she was living not in chronos time—"the poor you will always have with you"—but in kairos time—"you will not always have me." In a fallen world, there will always be the pain of life. Injustice, disease, prejudice, despair, these will always be with us. Opportunity to deal with issues of poverty will always be present. Not until God's kingdom comes will we have a perfect world with no social and economic disparity.

Here was a woman who understood that what is appropriate at one time and place may not be appropriate at another time and place. Jesus calls us to respond to the challenges of our day in ways that are appropriate to the time we are given. The right moment for doing certain things quickly passes. Incarnations are fleeting. Here was the Incarnate God in the flesh in their midst, yet only one person recognized him and his mission.

She is a model disciple. She seizes the opportunity created by Jesus' presence. Unlike Peter, she denies herself for Jesus' sake. In contrast to the rich man, she sacrifices her valued possessions. When reproached, she remains silent. In the face of death—the death of Jesus—she is neither afraid nor sorrowful nor self-absorbed. In the anointing of Jesus as king in his death, she shows that she is the first person, apart from Jesus, to perceive the crucial importance of the Passion.

—STEPHEN C. BARTON

Here was a woman who, in the midst of guile and malice by the scribes and Pharisees, plots by eight chief priests, and empty promises by twelve chief disciples, threw confidence and caution to the wind and emptied her heart and wallet, allowing herself to become a fool for love. Any wonder the disciples were so angry? Any wonder when Jesus rebuked the disciples saying, "Let her alone . . . why do you make trouble for her?" They almost lost it? One did lose it. The Gospel story continues in verse 10 by inferring that Jesus made Judas so mad by defending this woman that Judas went out and betrayed him.

The smell of that perfume—the burial anointing—was the last straw for Judas.

Messiah literally means "the Anointed One." There were diverse, even conflicting understandings and ideas of messiahship, but one thing was sure: the term "the Anointed One" was in common use as the designation of the man whom God was expected to make king of his people at the end times. By pouring this oily perfume over Jesus' head, this woman symbolically proclaimed him to be the Messiah, the Anointed One of God.

Jesus is anointed Messiah, not by a king, potentate, or priest, but by an insignificant woman; not in the temple of the holy city, but in the house of a leper in a lowly town called Bethany.

How long did the scent of that fragrance linger?

How's your sense of smell? When you were born, the mechanism of your nose was capable of detecting and identifying ten thousand different scents. How much of this sensory capacity have you developed? Or how many of us are functionally "anosmic," or without a sense of smell. Some people are born anosmic, others have developed anosmia from head injuries. Still others have drifted into anosmic states of being by repressing their sense of smell.

Two years ago, *The New York Times* commemorated Valentines Day by doing a "Science Times" feature spread on what it called "the second-sexiest organ of the body"—the nose. It seems that the odor receptors of the nose are more sophisticated and complex than either the eye or the ear. In fact, the nose may be the sense organ leading fastest to the brain. There is an immediate link-up between nose and brain. Odor information works on the brain directly, unlike the indirect route taken by auditory and visual. Also unlike the other nerve cells, olfactory neurons regenerate.

Each person has an odor-print that is as characteristic as a thumbprint or voiceprint.

HOW DOES a sperm wend its way toward an egg? Odor receptors.

HOW DOES an infant find its mother's nipple? Smell.

HOW DOES a mother pick out her newborn from other newborns? Smell.

You've heard beauty is in the eye of the beholder. It's even more accurate to say that odor is in the nose of the smeller! Biologist Lewis Thomas and media philosopher Marshall McLuhan first suggested this in the early 1970s. In 1974, Thomas argued that our genes give off a certain odor, and that people are attracted to those whose genes smell most unlike their own.

McLuhan, in conjunction with his nephew, chemist Ross Hall, announced in 1971 the patent of a formula for the removal of urine odor from undergarments. Registered under the trademark Prohtex, McLuhan's compound removed the one odor without obliterating other smells, such as perspiration. In the aural and tactile environment of preliterate man, McLuhan explained, body odor had been (and still is in some parts of the world) a prime method of communication. He predicted that in the global village created by electronic technology, tribal odors would make a comeback as well.

The psalmist hints that God can smell a proud person from a long ways away: "The proud he knows from afar" (Ps. 138:6 NKJV). Isaiah says explicitly that there is a stench or a stink to a proud person. Is it possible that different spirits have different odors? Can't you smell in someone the aroma of arrogance and pride? What about the aroma of humility and obedience?

Now scientists around the world are proving both McLuhan and Thomas right. Claus Wedekind, a zoologist at Bern University in Switzerland, has tested women's responses to sweaty T-shirts and found that they have definite opinions. He first asked women to rate T-shirts as pleasant or unpleasant at the midpoint of their menstrual cycles (when their noses are allegedly the keenest). What he found is that women are most attracted to the smell of men who are most unlike them in the immune system genes known as MHC genes. Once a woman got pregnant, however, she preferred the odor of people with similar MHC gene odors. Now the issue is not mate choice but help choice, and relatives are deemed the most helpful.

According to Wedekind, MHC plays a role in more than the selection of a mate. MHC prevents inbreeding as well as boosts immune functioning. The more diverse the MHC, the more effective in stopping pathogens. Choosing MHC-dissimilar mates may, therefore, serve three ends: increasing fertility, producing hardier offspring, and reducing the risk of genetic disease.

Or take another study conducted at the University of Chicago hospitals, where geneticist Carole Ober keeps a five-decades file of records on the North American Hutterites, from which she is exploring the relationship between genetics and fertility. Ober has discovered that mothers are more likely to abort spontaneously a fetus whose human leukocyte antigens (HLA) are the same as her own. In other words, mothers favor fetuses different from themselves, preserving genetic variability and the survival of the species.

Ober also discovered that mates favor those with different combinations of HLA from their own. How do they do it? Studies with mice have demonstrated that during infancy, mice learn to avoid mates with their parents' HLA types, and they do so by smell. Ober isn't ready yet to say that humans smell out their mates; she can't find the mechanism in humans by which they decide which mates to avoid. But she does claim that "people do discriminate on smell a lot more than we are aware," pointing to companies that are beginning to market pheromone perfumes.

Preaching without spiritual aroma is like a nose without fragrance.
We can only get the perfume by getting more of Christ.

—A. B. SIMPSON

Robert A. Heinlein states in his novel *Job A Comedy of Justice* (1984) that religion is the most prevalent drive in the human species, and that when it is present you can literally smell it.

The ancient Hebrews believed they could smell God's presence in the incense (which the Mexicans called "cigarettes for the gods"). Exodus 30:1–5 (cf. 37:25–28) instructed that an altar of incense was to be placed in front of the veil, and perpetual incense was to be offered by the priests night and morning. Exodus 30:6 even may mean that the altar of incense was within the veil, or within the Holy of Holies itself (cf. Heb. 9:4).

Of all our sensory amnesia in the modern era, we have done the most to trivialize and neutralize our sense of smell. It's not just that we've removed the smell from our worship (in the form of candles or incense). We're so afraid of smell, we've repressed it through flush toilets, cordoned-off sewage farms, catalytic converters, industrial zoning, aromatherapy, prisons, homeless shelters, and isolation wings of hospitals and old folks' homes. Even our gardens have been designed for the eye instead of the nose. It is only in the past decade that there has been a move to bring back floral fragrances in the garden and restore high scents to our homes. For the first time in many decades, "professional and amateur gardeners alike are again viewing flowers with an eye to the nose," observes Sally Ferguson of the Netherlands Flower Bulb Information Center.

And yet the odor of sanctity has not disappeared entirely. A minister friend from Indiana, Terry Rhine, tells of going into the sanctuary after everyone has left the church on Sunday morning and just sitting there savoring the lingering sweet smell of God's people at worship.

In his afterward to the twentieth anniversary edition of his 1976 classic, *The Cultural Contradictions of Capitalism*, Daniel Bell wrote, "It is striking that in every major city in the world, from New York to Helsinki to Tokyo, every large department store one enters displays cosmetics and fragrances spread across its ground floor." Bell sees this as evidence that the tension between "asceticism and acquisitiveness" has been resolved in favor of acquisitiveness. But might not the perfume industry, a $6 billion-a-year business, suggest something other than the frivolity of acquisitiveness?

Why is the smell of popcorn so memorable? Freshly popped popcorn conveys twenty-three key odor compounds with fragrances reminiscent of cloves, mushrooms, caramel, vanilla, roast potatoes, cooked apples, and fried fat.

There are two things we know about this least developed, most mysterious of all our senses, this most postmodern sense of smell: fragrances affect our moods, and are an almost infallible trigger of memory.

The sense of smell is wired in the brain to our emotions. Things that smell good just may be good for you. My mother used to put some camphor and rosemary in a pot of hot water and make me inhale the steam. It smelled good, but it also cleared out my sinuses. While aromatherapy (or essential oils therapy) is debatable, the ability of pleasant fragrances to elevate people's moods and enhance creativity is scientifically proven. The scent of a room can stimulate energy as much as a verbal compliment. Fragrances influence behavior, too—chamomile or lavender for relaxation, frankincense or nutmeg and lavender to relieve stress, lemon and peppermint as stimulants, geranium for mood swings, or a mixture of the essential oils of rosemary and lemon to heighten concentration.

To distinguish it from "aromatherapy," the study of the impact of scents on the mind and spirit is being called "aromacology." Japan has already put aromas in the workplace by pumping in scents through the air conditioning system. Lemon wakes employees up in the morning, rose calms them during lunch, tree-trunk oil helps them through the pit in the afternoon. One study of keypunch operators indicated that when the office air was scented with lavender, the number of errors per hour dropped by 21 percent; a jasmine fragrance produced a 33 percent error reduction, and the rate dropped by 54 percent when a lemon scent was used. However, with the lemon scent, work also slowed down, which may mean that the fragrance relaxes while simultaneously making workers more alert.

"Fragrance is decorating's fifth dimension," says an executive from Demeter Fragrances, one of many companies counting on environmental fragrancing in the very near future. In places where repetitive chores induce stress, why not pump in peppermint scents? Lace bedrooms with lavender to foster sleep; perfume MRIs with heliotropin (vanilla) to ease patient anxiety during medical diagnostic procedures.

Researchers at the Smell and Taste Treatment and Research Foundation in Chicago have created an artificial floral scent that, in preliminary tests, accelerates the rate of learning by as much as 150 percent. According to Dr.

Alan Hirsch, neurological director of the foundation, the scent greatly enhanced retention when sprayed in a room where study participants completed tasks such as finding their way through a maze. The potential ramifications of the findings are substantial.

> Fragrance is decorating's fifth dimension.
> —EXECUTIVE, DEMETER FRAGRANCES

"The [scent] theory works in the classroom or in employee training," says Dr. Hirsch. Why not in our homes and entertainment centers? Three decades ago Hollywood tried "Smell-O-Vision," a machine at the back of each theater that released a hissing, perfumy odor that matched the plot line in the film. There is now a parody page of this ill-fated movie-going experience on the Web, put there by Agency.com, a New York-based Web marketing firm (see www.realaroma.com). The Web page is meant as parody, but look at it as prophecy. Already the home fragrance business alone has become a $950 million-a-year industry. Crayola crayons are now coming scented—orange smells like orange, blue supposedly smells like fresh air, etc. Walt Disney World in Florida already uses smell in its ride Pirates of the Caribbean, which features the faint odor of smoldering timbers. The latest diet gimmick? An aversion therapy called "AromaTrim," which connects a food you abuse to a stench. Every time you binge, you sniff a cartridge that smells of something between vomit and gym socks.

Perhaps more mysterious than scent's capability to alter moods is its ability to conjure up memories from the past. Some scientists believe that smell is the most powerful releaser of memory there is! The science of "olfactory-evoked recall" is the study of the ability of scents to transport people to pleasant faces and places. Smells are the "presences" that create "absences." Smell chalk, and most people will recall school days memories that are good. One whiff and an entire episode in one's past is brought back to mind. To this day my favorite shampoos are balsam-based because some of my most wonderful memories of growing up took place at Pine Grove Camp Meeting outside of Saratoga Springs, New York. When I open balsam shampoo and sniff its boreal fragrance, I have opened a chest full of camp meeting memories, releasing into my life the smell of family, home-cooked meals, sawdust trails, shouting Methodists, teenage dates, and furtive kisses behind brush arbors.

My shower always contains another "Muzak for the nose," the coconut-scented Nexxus Moisturizing Therappe Shampoo. Whenever I bring this shampoo to lather on my head, I bathe my being in memories of wonderful times with my oldest son at Newcomb Hollow Beach near South Wellfleet, Cape Cod. I used to use a coconut-scented suntan oil to protect his baby skin from the sun, and to this day that smell brings back the sight, sound, and fragrance of the sun-bathed sand and tide.

In talking with others about their favorite fragrances, I have discovered there are regional differences to what our sense of scent conjures up. East Coast folks prefer floral scents, and Northerners, the smell of the seasons. Southerners seem to prefer hearty snorts of pine, while Midwesterners like the whiff of hay and farm animals. Westerners like the aroma of barbecued meat. Whatever our pet smell, huge histories of time are relived within the microseconds of a sniff. Nothing can bring back a time, a place, or an emotion better than an aroma.

 There is no odor so bad as that which arises from goodness tainted.

—HENRY DAVID THOREAU

One day I was getting ready to preach. The song leader asked everyone to be seated and to sing meditatively the old song, "Ivory Palaces." As I sat there in that modern ivory palace, singing how Jesus came "Out of the ivory palaces, into this world of woe," it suddenly hit me that Jesus left the smells of pearly gates, streets of gold, walls of jasper and other precious stones, and the fragrance of holiness for the smells of planet Earth.

Jesus entered this world smelling what? A stable, a barnyard.

Jesus left this world smelling what?

The Israelites didn't take baths every day. They washed their hands frequently (before every meal), but they washed their bodies even less often than the Egyptians. In Jesus' day, there were Jewish aristocrats living in upper Jerusalem who had in their houses baths for purification called *mikvaot*. But Jesus was not one of the wealthy, nor did his sense of purity agree with the upscale Jewish establishment.

The smell stayed with him.

We need to remember one thing about crucifixion. The science of torture has never equaled, much less excelled, that Roman practice of crucifixion, and the crucifixion of Jesus of Nazareth was no exception.

Crucifixion was more than an ugliness blotted out by Easter, more than a speed bump on the road to resurrection. Part of the cruelty of crucifixion was the emotional as well as physical torture. Yes, Jesus' physical agonies were beyond imagining. But the emotional agonies were even worse. Emotional agonies that attended the humiliation of being stripped naked, with all body parts and functions exposed for the humiliating gaze of the public; the mixture of blood and sweat and urine and feces creating a nauseating stench; the smells of extinction, that kept even the families of the crucified at a distance.

But what cut even deeper were the agonies of the spirit. The Bible unabashedly testifies to Jesus' sense of total abandonment, defeat, rejection, and betrayal. In many ways, this was where Jesus was really crucified in spirit. Not on the cross, but in the kiss.

The cross crucified him in body. The kiss crucified him in soul. He was truly despised and rejected, a man of sorrows, acquainted with grief.

Jesus was really betrayed twice. First by the kiss of Judas, then by something that cut even deeper than that kiss: the kiss-off by Peter. The disciple who stuck with Jesus the longest after his arrest, who defended him with a sword in the garden . . . when accosted by a servant girl in the courtyard of the high priest, denied he knew Jesus. When the barnyard cock crowed, the second betrayal took place.

Now do you know why Jesus said to remember her?

In the Praetorium at Pilate's residence, the soldiers decked Jesus in royal clothes like some play doll. They draped over him a scarlet robe and stuck some reeds into his hands to mock a scepter—and then used that instrument to bludgeon Jesus on the head.

They beat him about the head with their hands and took turns spitting into the contusions of his blindfolded face. They knelt before him and taunted, "Hail, King of the Jews!" Then they crushed onto his head that crown of thorns.

With blood, spittle, and sweat running down his face, Jesus looked around . . . where were his disciples? Where were all of his faithful followers?

Where were all of those whom Jesus had healed? Where were all those whose eyes he had opened, whose ears he had unstopped, whose mouths he had opened, whose limbs he had restored?

It was almost more than he could bear.

But then Jesus smelled the perfume, the spikenard that had anointed his head only hours before . . .

And when he remembered the woman with the hemorrhage of twelve years, who had faith to reach out and touch the hem of his garment and be healed;

And when they beat him with a whip until the blood ran down his back like a waterfall, his skin already supersensitive from the aftereffects of hematidrosis (sweating blood);

And when they put back his own clothes onto his raw skin;

And when they marched him 650 yards through the streets;

And when they made him climb the Via Dolorosa carrying the 150-pound patibulum on which his wrists were later to be nailed, reducing him to a beast of burden being led to the slaughter;

And when the weight of the cross produced contusions of the right shoulder and back;

And when he fell, causing more unnamed injuries;

And when he looked around for his most intimate friends, his disciples, and saw none but the four women and John at a distance;

And when the agony was almost too much to bear;

Then Jesus smelled the perfume.

And when he remembered the twelve-year-old daughter of Jairus, whom everyone thought was dead but whom God had healed when he had spoken these words, "Get up, my child";

And when they stripped him naked and nailed him to the crosspiece he had carried;

And when they took those six-inch spikes and lacerated his median nerves in his hands and feet to the cross;

And when they lifted him up on that Tau cross above the stinking garbage heap called Golgotha;

And when everyone who passed by mocked him on the cross, when the chief priests and scribes, even those who were crucified with him, taunted and teased him in his agony;

And when the only thing the soldiers offered this dying, crucified man was a drink of vinegar, which could only increase his unspeakable agony;

And when the loneliness became so severe he was about ready to give up;

And when he remembered the many children brought to him by their mothers, children who sat on his lap and eagerly listened to his stories;

And when his tormentors used him for entertainment, "Let's see if he can call down the angels";

Then Jesus looked around . . .

. . . and smelled the perfume.

And when, with his body already in shock, hanging from his wrists, he was only able to breathe in, unable to breathe out;

And when he struggled for breath, unable to gasp even small hiccups of air without straightening his knees and raising himself on the fulcrum of his nailed feet;

And when he searched the landscape for signs of love and faithfulness, and realized he was abandoned by nearly everyone he loved;

Jesus cried out, "My God, My God, why have you forsaken me!"

And even this wail was mocked by those who mistook his cry to God as a cry to Elijah, and waited to make sure Elijah didn't come so they could mock him some more.

Then Jesus, with precious little breath left, smelled the perfume.

And he remembered this woman who gave all she had that he would remember God's love for him, and in that smell even detect the odors that told him he was going home from whence he came.

 The greatest of these is love.
—THE APOSTLE PAUL

The greatest honor anyone can give anyone is to tell their story. Here was someone who "did what she could," literally, she "used what she had."

Will you?

Will we?

Now do you know why Jesus said, "When you remember me, remember her"?

Chapter 11
NO FEAR!

Fear not, I am with thee,
O be not dismayed, For I am thy God and
will still give thee aid;
I'll strengthen and help thee,
and cause thee to stand upheld by
my righteous, omnipotent hand.
—"How Firm a Foundation"

Remember when you were growing up? Could you paint a bad picture? Didn't you love your own artwork? Whether executed at school, at home, or in the yard, didn't you run to your parents with the paint dripping wet to show it off, eager to hear the magic words, "Let's hang it up"? Once your artwork achieved pride of place on the art gallery wall—which in every home seems to be the refrigerator door—you were hurt to ever find it missing. I'll never forget my horror as a child at finding one of my masterpieces in the wastepaper basket. No matter it had been hanging on the fridge for six months; no matter the paper was turning yellow; no matter the paint was chipping off onto the linoleum. It was a great picture and deserved better.

By the time I went to junior high, I wouldn't show anyone my drawings. I hadn't stopped drawing, but I kept them to myself. By the time I went to college, I wouldn't even draw. I was embarrassed at how bad an artist I was, or perceived I was. At the University of Richmond, where I double-majored in history and psychology, I was assigned to study the "HTP" Inventory in a psych course on Principles of Psychological Testing. HTP stands for "House-Tree-Person," and I remember pleading with the professor to assign a different psychological test, to exempt me from the exercise, because my houses, trees, and persons were so awful I didn't want anyone to see them.

What happened between ages four and fourteen, between four and twenty? Or let me put the question in a larger cultural framework: What turns a four-year-old munchkin into a fourteen-year-old murderer?

What happened to me is that I learned the awesome power of FUD (fear, uncertainty, doubt). What happened is I learned that there were such things as "bad drawings." What happened is I learned that there were such things as "bad questions." What happened is I learned a four-letter word: *fear*. When I was a child, I drew with *no fear*. I fearlessly drew from my inner spirit, and trusted that they would be good and beautiful and true. But as I grew older, I learned to fear—to fear the wild things within, fear the comparisons and judgments of others, fear the self-revelation, fear my own weaknesses.

Go to the London National Gallery and see the *Adoration of the Magi* painting by Botticelli. Visit Leningrad and see the *Portrait of Madame Matisse* painting by Matisse. Both Matisse and Botticelli paint people with some very exaggerated features, but they paint that way because every line they draw, they accept from God. Every twist and turn of the brush, they receive as an inspired gift. They paint with *no fear*, and what they paint comes out beautiful.

You've heard Lord Acton's famous phrase, "Power corrupts, and absolute power corrupts absolutely." I can name a four-letter word that corrupts more than power. The word is *fear*. Fear corrupts the world, fear corrupts the church, more than power does. Granted, it is not easy to make sense of the "moronic inferno" of contemporary North American culture, to quote Saul

Bellow; but whatever tack one takes, we are living in a culture of fear. Our faith communities are especially suffering from fear fever, and are desperately looking for health insurance protection rather than prevention and cure. The two most important words for every one of us to confront are these words: *fear* and *trust*. What words will we wrap around these two words?

There is a reason for the title of Francis Fukuyama's follow-up to his bestseller *End of History*. The title of this sequel is one word: *TRUST*.

There is a reason why the computer game "Myst" quickly became the number one CD-ROM game of 1994. It's fundamental question: *Who can you trust?*

There is a reason why Fox Television's *The X-Files*, which beat out *ER*, *NYPD Blue*, and *Chicago Hope* for a Golden Globe Award as the best dramatic series in 1994, flashed these words on the screen at the beginning of each early episode: "Trust No One. Fear Everything."

The times we live in are infiltrated with a pervasive climate of fear. We're driven by the "Fear Thing." We fear to go out at night on quiet walks through city parks. We fear to allow our children to walk home from school in broad daylight. We fear the Net, where porn lurks to undermine our homes. We fear television programming, in case some unstable person gets a perverted idea and acts it out in the real world.

The Fear Thing is dominating the screen, from *Outbreak* to *Casper*, from *X-Files* to *Buffy, the Vampire Slayer*. Ambrose Bierce defines a "ghost" as "an outward and visible sign of an inward fear." Our fears, however individual, are basically all the same, and our attraction to fear can only be explained as the Fear Thing.

The Fear Thing is dominating politics, from Rush Limbaugh to H. Ross Perot. There have always been citizens who feared their government. But this Fear Thing is now at a point some are calling "fusion paranoia"—a meeting of the extreme right and extreme left who join hands in their common fear of government, a fear that is now shared by over 50 percent of our nation's people—from paramilitary groups to ordinary citizens. Look at Timothy McVeigh on the right and the Unabomber on the left. The paranoia of the right brought Oklahoma City to its knees, while the paranoia of the left galvanized one of the world's largest airports—LAX—in fear.

The Fear Thing is dominating our need for security. Just look at our cars to see the security issue at work. First we install seat belts. Then we install shoulder belts. Then we build contraptions that put both together. Then we turn the shoulder harness into a boa constrictor that pins us to our seats and doesn't let us move. Then we install air bags. Pretty soon we'll be riding around inside a giant marshmallow.

We could go through the same security exercise with alarms—car, smoke, carbon monoxide, burglar, radon, etc. We're alarmed to the teeth! Everybody is scrambling for security—protect yourself from criminals, from electronic looters, from car-jackers. And what is propelling the sale of car phones? Security. Our nation has a security force in which there are more private police officers than public police officers. We are living in a culture where, when the President of the U.S. announces he will put 100,000 more police officers on our streets, we open our mouths and breathe a sigh of relief.

The Fear Thing is dominating our relationships. Just ask any African-American male walking across a stoplighted intersection about the sound of automatic car door locks suddenly snapping shut.

The Fear Thing is dominating our childrearing practices. From their earliest moments we raise our children in a school of fear. I don't mean by this that their schools are filled with fear, although they are. Nearly 75 percent of junior high and high school students polled in 1994 said that violence and crime is a "major problem" among teenagers. They say they are living in fear. Even though the crime rate may be going down, our children's fear rate is going up. By "school of fear" I mean more deeply the atmosphere in which our children live and move and have their being. One of the earliest lessons we teach our children is to fear strangers. A 1987 Roper poll found that 76 percent of our children feared being kidnapped. In fact, it was their number one concern. Rummaging through the old magazines in a physician's waiting room not too long ago, I found an article in the October 1994 issue of *Family Life*. The title says it all: "What to Do When a Stranger Says Hello?"

And what do we teach our kids about Mother Nature? We teach them about environmental degradation, the collapse of the ecosystem, etc. In other words, we create an atmosphere of fear and despair to get our kids to love their planet and develop an environmental ethic. Is it any wonder buster teenagers clutch bottled water like boomer infants clung to bottled milk? These are the words of Mike Weilbacher, president of the Pennsylvania Alliance for Environmental Education:

> Our children are convinced that the ozone hole will soon fry them, global warming will soon flood them, garbage will bury them alive, and rain forest fires will suffocate them as oxygen vanishes. They believe they will inhabit a planet free of pandas, gorillas, whales, condors, tigers, and just about any creature of majesty or mystery. In fact, many kids are convinced they won't even reach adulthood, for there won't even be an earth by then. When they should be celebrating the beauty of life, they instead are told to mourn its loss. Just as they are being introduced to nature, they are told to bid it farewell. And worse, they are told to hate themselves for wreaking this ecological apocalypse, and even revile us, their parents.

We even fear our food! An article appeared recently in the *Atlanta Journal* titled, "Fear of Food." It was written by an infectious disease physician and a dietician chronicling their daughter's bout with E. coli, confessing that even with their medical expertise, they could not protect their daughter from this infection. They now live in fear of food.

> No one must
> pass by without my knowing
> where he's going,
> what she's doing . . .
> For my life, give me
> all lives,
> Give me all the sorrow
> of all the world and
> I will transform it
> into hope.
>
> —CHALDEAN NERUDA PABLO NERUDA

Fear is the number one problem facing the world today.
What is at the core of racism? Fear.
What is at the core of sexism? Fear.

What is at the core of outsider-immigration hysteria? Fear.

What is at the core of why more and more of us are packing guns? Fear.

What is at the core of why more and more road warriors are packing cellular phones? Fear.

What is at the core of why people will stay in a job they hate for a lifetime? Fear.

What is at the core of why parents find it increasingly necessary to attach harnesses to their children in shopping malls? Fear.

What is at the core of why liberals and conservatives battle to gain control of the public arena? Fear.

What is at the core of why many school children are met each morning by metal detectors and armed security guards or police officers before they can be educated? Fear.

A certain passage from Scripture, John 21:1–14, addresses our Fear Thing in a revealing way. It is a story that takes place after Jesus' resurrection. It used to be that this chapter was seen as an add-on, an appendix or epilogue, that somehow got tacked onto the end of John's Gospel. Recently scholars are seeing it as cumulative and culminative.

After these things Jesus showed Himself again to the disciples at the Sea of Tiberias, and in this way He showed Himself: Simon Peter, Thomas called Didymus, Nathanael of Cana in Galilee, the sons of Zebedee, and two others of His disciples were together. Simon Peter said to them, "I am going fishing." They said to him, "We are going with you also." They went out and immediately got into the boat, and that night they caught nothing. But when the morning had now come, Jesus stood on the shore; yet the disciples did not know that it was Jesus. Then Jesus said to them, "Children, have you any food?"

They answered Him, "No."

And He said to them, "Cast the net on the right side of the boat, and you will find some." So they cast, and now they were not able to draw it in because of the multitude of fish.

Therefore that disciple whom Jesus loved said to Peter, "It is the Lord!" Now when Simon Peter heard that it was the Lord, he put on his outer

garment (for he had removed it), and plunged into the sea. But the other
disciples came in the little boat (for they were not far from land, about two
hundred cubits), dragging the net with fish. Then, as soon as they had
come to land, they saw a fire of coals there, and fish laid on it, and bread.
Jesus said to them, "Bring some of the fish which you have just caught."
Simon Peter went up and dragged the net to land, full of large fish, one
hundred and fifty-three; and although there were so many, the net was not
broken. Jesus said to them, "Come and eat breakfast."
Yet none of the disciples dared ask Him, "Who are you?"—
knowing that it was the Lord. Jesus then came and took the bread
and gave it to them, and likewise the fish.
This is now the third time Jesus showed Himself to His disciples after
He was raised from the dead.

—JOHN 21:1–14 NKJV

The disciples had most likely returned to their old trades. Seven of them
returned to fishing, led by Peter's example. When Peter said, "I am going
away fishing," this is not like you or I saying, "I'm going for a car ride,"
rather it's like you or I saying, "I give up!" The disciples felt like they had literally lived a dream, a dream of a Messiah that was now over, and there was
nowhere to go but back to the way things used to be before meeting this
man, Jesus. But life is never that easy. "That night they caught nothing."
They fished in vain, and didn't know why. Life is often empty and the
nights, long and lonely. But morning comes, and with the dawn, joy. Jesus
stood on the beach, watching them as they exhaustedly, frustratedly headed
for shore. They did not see him, or if they did, they did not recognize him.
It is often hard to recognize Jesus if we are not keenly looking for him,
because sometimes he comes unawares.

As that stranger looked on, he asked the ancient question, "Catch anything?" More literally, "Do you have any *prosfagion?*" which means trim-
mings or morsels. They growled back, "No," still not recognizing Jesus. He
recommended they cast their nets from the other side of the boat. Jesus' leadership was based not on fear, but compassion. He didn't say, "Do you want
to go hungry?" "Do you want to go home empty handed?" Instead, he told

them to change their methodology and cast from the other side. In other words, reenter life again from another angle.

The Santa Fe Institute for Nonlinear Studies is studying what it calls "complex adaptive systems." These are systems that respond through nonlinear dynamics and feedback loops that are both analytical (takes apart) and synthetic (puts together) to the conditions and contexts they are in by exploring and exploiting them. In this situation, Jesus is saying that his disciples should become a complex adaptive system. You know the disciples must have protested. You also know exactly what they said.

- We've never done it that way before.

- We tried that before and it didn't work.

- No respectable fisherman casts nets that way.

- It's too radical a change for us.

- Oh, if it only were that easy!

- When you've been around longer, you'll understand why it can't be done that way.

- How dare a stranger criticize what we're doing.

- We've been running this place long before you came around.

- What you're suggesting is against our policy.

- Won't that open us up to liability?

- Who made you God?

- We aren't crazy, why would we do that?

Ted Koppel conducted an interview with a man who had been trapped on an oil rig during a fire. Koppel asked the man how he had the courage to jump from a platform fifteen stories high into water engulfed in flames. The man replied, "Because I was going to fry if I stayed on the platform!"

That's what makes us jump. The platform we have been living on and doing ministry on is crumbling under our feet, and we are forced to cast our nets from the other side.

For whatever reason, whether they were too tired to protest, or they were totally desperate for things to be different—they take the stranger's advice. With what results? The outcome was beyond anyone's imagination! Success came from the obedience of Peter and the other disciples to the words of Jesus. They found more fish than they ever had, and what's more, the net held, even with such a large catch.

John Calvin in his commentary on this verse says that "Christ showed His power, first in their taking so large a draught of fishes, and secondly, when by His hidden power He preserved the net which must otherwise have been torn and burst." Notice, the disciples only recognized Christ when their nets were so full of fish they couldn't haul them on board. Finally, one disciple said to Peter, "It is the Lord!" Jesus was recognized, not by his words, not by his appearance, not even by his voice. Jesus was recognized by his impact on other people's lives. Jesus is known by the magic of his transforming touch.

These words, "cast your nets from the other side," are medicine for our times. Why are we so resistant to change?

Sometimes it's fear to be ourselves, to follow our spiritual instincts. In the movie, *Forrest Gump*, Jenny asks, "What you gonna be when you grow up?" and Forrest says, "Why can't I be me?" This is one of the hardest things in the world to do.

A big tourist attraction in central Florida is the motion picture studio in Orlando. One of its departments is called "Central Casting." This is the place where they coordinate the actors and actresses who play the extras and bit roles in the movies. One day a novice actor appeared on a set to do a stand-in part. The director setting up the shot called him over. "Who are you?" the director asked. The young actor obligingly gave his name. "I don't want your name, what character are you playing?" The actor hemmed and hawed, and then confessed he wasn't quite sure. Finally the exasperated director shouted back, "You'd better call central casting and find out who you are!"

How many of us need to call home and find out once again who we are? God made each of us different. If God loves difference so much, why is difference, why is living, such a liability in the church? When Moses had his mid-life crisis, he fled to the desert, became a shepherd, and began to spend time with God. It was in the midst of his mid-life crisis that he learned to be himself; it was not achievement or activities but relationship with God that constituted for him a fruitful life.

> Almost always it is the fear of being ourselves that brings us to the mirror.
> —ANTONIO PORCHIA

Another common fear is that our nets won't hold. Are you haunted by the prospect that you may not be able to handle all those fish even if you caught them? Do you repeatedly say, "Nothing fails like success"?

The disciples were afraid of success. They had the fear of closing. After his resurrection, Jesus' disciples were not looking for a living Christ; they were looking for a dead Christ. Are we truly expecting God to do what God says? When God did, like in the case of the man who was healed of his demons, the people were scared stiff (Luke 8:26). As long as the man was crazy, everybody was fine; as soon as the man was "clothed and in his right mind," the people became fearful.

By *success* I am not using the word as the world defines the term. Do you want to turn things around? Then turn things upside-down! Our definition of *success* needs to be turned upside-down. As Jesus turned the tables of the temple upside-down in his temple tantrum, so he turns the tables on every one of our definitions of success.

Are you better at working solo than working as a team? Are you afraid of surrendering some of your control and power to others? Net fishing is a team effort. You can't do it by yourself. How did Jesus send his followers out to take on the world? In teams. "I can't be me without you" is one of my life mantras. We need each other. Most especially, we need Christ. As the disciples found out, apart from Christ we can do nothing (John 15:5). They caught nothing that night. Without Jesus' help, they fished in vain. Disciples of Jesus never catch anything without the help of Jesus.

Net fishing is best done with a team of experts who will diminish their own interests for the sake of the success of the team. The ideal team is a team of harmonious difference; not where like meets like, but where difference meets difference. Just as genetic diversity is imperative to the survival of any ecosystem, so pluraformity is imperative to the success of any endeavor. The difference between pluraformity and pluralism? In pluraformity, there are wide divergences around a common core; in pluralism, there is no core and no connections, only centrifuge. The experience of Pentecost—the reversal of Babel—empowers us to recognize and respect differences so that, in Paul's words, "We may be strengthened in the faith, I by yours and you by mine."

The business world has been teaching us that a large part of being the best is working with the best; a large part of being the best is positioning people to be just as good, if not better, than you. Teamwork is more than a corporate fad and fix, although I admit at times to thinking that the business world has overdosed on teams. But one look at the McDonald's empire, and I quickly back down. How does McDonald's get minimum wage employees to work full time when there is a vast shortage of labor for minimum-wage jobs? They invite people to join "The McDonald's Team."

Why aren't we inviting people to join "The Jesus Team"?

It is perfectly possible to laugh over injustice until we cry—and it is equally possible to laugh amidst injustice until we suffer—in ridiculous delight at the existence that, however painful, it is nevertheless ours.

—WILLIAM BIRMINGHAM

Are you afraid that others will laugh at what you're doing? Do you fear the laughter of others who wouldn't think of casting their nets from that side of the boat? Can you hear them laughing right now?

In the words of one consultant speaking at a workshop on racial discrimination, "Who's in charge of whether or not you are offended by something someone says? That's right . . . *you* are! If you choose to give up your power to another and allow them to push your buttons, go right ahead. But don't for one minute pretend it's anyone's decision but yours." You can just as easily offend somebody simply by walking into the room. Should you not go into the room? How people respond to us is up to them. But our response to the world is up to us.

Afraid of change? There is a difference between change that steps up to the times and change that keeps in step with the times, change that keeps us in touch with the culture while staying in tune with the Spirit, and change that keeps us in tune with the culture while staying in touch with the Spirit. It's not as if there isn't a good reason for this fear of change. When change is doubling every year, that's a lot of change to handle—that's almost violent change. But when we have trouble handling even basic change . . .

My all-time favorite change-a-light-bulb joke is this one: Q: How many church members does it take to change a light bulb? A: Who said anything about "change"?

The *Journal of American Demographics* did a report on the conflicting attitudes of Americans to change, and gave it this title: "Change is Good, Unless It Happens." How many of us, how many of our churches, could put up that sign with pride, a sign that advertises our resistance to change? Change is not something that comes and goes, an event that happens, like a gust of wind. That's why the "winds of change" metaphor is misleading. Change is something that is constant; it never comes and goes, but always is. When Paul said "I am dying daily," he was admitting that he was changing daily. Change is as constant and as natural as breathing.

Do a little exercise. Put your hand up to your chin and breathe out hard. What do you feel on your hand? Your breath? Not exactly. What you feel is your liver vanishing into thin air, your lungs being exhaled right before your very eyes, your intestines getting new lining. And what you are breathing in is the body parts of others that are now becoming part of you (and you wondered why it is that married couples start to look like one another after the years!).

Our bodies are undergoing such constant change that you are a totally new person every five to seven years. A man's cells have all been replaced in that length of time (it takes a woman seven years to become a totally new person because of some recalcitrant reproductive cells). One of the mysteries of consciousness is this: Can you remember yourself ten years ago? Fifteen years ago? Then you are remembering somebody who isn't there any longer. You are now two people removed from that person you are remembering. Have any of you women been married twenty-five years? If so, then you're no different from the Samaritan woman at the well. You too have had five husbands—each different, with a whole new set of cellular apparatus.

The truth is, the more set our routines of life become, the more we resist change. As more sand falls into the lower half of my hourglass than is left in the top, I am finding out the reality of what has been called "a hardening of the *oughteries*." Or to reconstruct the issue in more proper terms, am I going to have an LTC (low threshold for change) or an HTC (high threshold to change) life? One of the most important junctions one comes to in the journey through life is that place where one must decide whether one is going to take the road of defending old positions or the road of making new discoveries. It is a juncture at which we stand every single day. Are you willing to get on roads you've never been on? Are you willing to take roads that lead you to places unknown? Or have you decided not to go anywhere you haven't been before?

To stay vibrantly alive one must have undiminished curiosity. Are you going to spend the rest of your life settling in to the set of assumptions and perspectives you already have? Or are you going to spend your life being stretched in new directions, exploring aspects of God you didn't even know were there?

One of the most hackneyed jokes in cartoons and comic strips is that of the bearded prophet, marching up and down the street carrying a sign, "The End Is Near." We laugh. We shake our heads. But sometimes the joke's on us; sometimes a Noah out there actually has been privy to a word from the Lord. The four horsemen of the twenty-first century apocalypse are: 1) disease, 2) violence, 3) environmental collapse, and 4) technological upheavals. Is there reason to fear?

THE DISEASE HORSE

The Doomsday Bug Hypothesis warns us that a plague is imminent. Bio-invasions of rapidly mutating, extremely contagious airborne "hot agents" or killer viruses are about to stalk the planet.

Those prophets carrying around this sign seem to be more right than we care to admit. At least a growing number of epidemiologists are beginning to carry the same placard after a sudden, terrifying outbreak of global epidemics. The 1995 meeting of the American Society for Microbiology warned of the very real threat of a "super-bug" that can't be stopped by any known antibiotics.

THE ENVIRONMENTAL HORSE

These riders of the apocalypse come in two guises. First is the belief that there is a giant asteroid out there with our name on it. Quite a bit of scientific evidence is available to confirm this hypothesis. Second is the belief that planet Earth is literally sick to death. The plants and animals of the world are dying; the ozone layer is vanishing. The nature of the earth's sickness is a cancer that is spreading across the globe like a can of Sherwin Williams paint. The cancer is called humans, and until the earth is freed from that cancer, another world like Noah once prophesied against is being born.

THE VIOLENCE HORSE

Jeremiah once had a vision (chap. 4) of a world that was falling apart, a world where the sky was falling, where everything that was good was falling away. The people of this world, Jeremiah sees in his vision, are "skilled in doing evil, but do not know how to do good" (Jer. 4:22).

Sound familiar? We are living in a world where some people have adopted the strategy, "If you can't beat 'em, shoot 'em." The ones who get shot may or may not have any relationship to the cause of the shooting, as the parents of neighborhood children struck down by random bullets can attest.

The increase in fear over violence is an evil that will match the violence itself. The fear of terrorism rides shotgun now with the fear of crime. The enemy within—fear—is just as powerful, and may become more powerful, than any enemy without.

THE TECHNOLOGY HORSE

In this bio-technological age, we are living in a Genesis-like world where nothing is predictable. Everything is up for grabs. And if one believes the evolutionary theory, one is tempted to conclude that humans are on the brink of kicking off a higher order of being that leaves us behind like we left the apes behind.

One writer of *Wired* magazine warns that the real force that will make humans extinct by the year 2088 is not the apocalyptic horses of flesh-eating bacteria, or rising seas, or rampaging violence, but the exponential growth of the integrated circuit. The computer is getting smarter and more adaptable than we are as a species. By the year 2088, Blonder argues, computers should match human intelligence. But this is not the real scare. "The scary thing is that this exponential curve keeps on going, and going, and going. By 2090, the computer will be twice as smart and twice as insightful as any human being. . . . By 2100, the gap will grow to the point at which homo sapiens, relatively speaking, might make a good pet. Then again, the computers of 2088 might not give us a second thought."

We democratic citizens [have] become more fearful than hopeful . . . a few of our most paralyzing collective fears: the next generation's way of life will not be better than that of previous generations; America's position in the world will falter; communities will continue to disintegrate; families will continue to collapse; the center simply will not hold. Fearful, we retreat or participate in the politics of resentment—finding somebody or some group to blame for all of our ills.

—Jean Pethke Elshtain

All this wonder and worry about the future is expressing itself in two ways, neither of which is healthy. First is nonchalance. In the 1997 smash-hit movie *Men in Black* there is an exchange between Will Smith and Tommy Lee Jones. Smith has just corralled another alien and reports his findings to Jones, "He said the world was coming to an end." Without a second's hesitation, Jones asks, "Did he say when?" Nero fiddled while Rome burned. We're playing the whole band while the world burns.

The second way our apocalyptic anxieties are manifesting themselves is in *fin de siecle* gloom and the crop of endist literature detailing and datelining doomsday, as our obsession with the end of time grows.

Yet in the midst of our fear and frozenness, this command comes to us: No Fear. On numerous occasions, Jesus spoke to the disciples and the crowd words that jar us from our paralysis and helplessness, "Fear no more!" And yet, we need to be careful; we are called to fear some things. "The fear of the Lord is the beginning of wisdom" Ps.111:10). Note that the Bible does not say the love of God is the beginning of wisdom, but the fear of God is the beginning of wisdom. Before no fear, we need to know fear.

One of the greatest Biblical definitions of the wicked is, in the words of the psalmist, one in whom "there is no fear of God before their eyes" (Ps. 36:1 NRSV). As our ancestors of ages past acknowledged in their marvelous compliments of "She's a God-fearing woman" or "He's a God-fearing man," we are supposed to fear God, respect him for who he is and what he can do. When we come before God's presence, *we had better have known fear*. Only in that way can we stand before the challenges of life with no fear.

Here are some situations that biblical figures found themselves in when the word of the Lord, "**NO FEAR**," came to them. Maybe you can identify with some of these personal circumstances:

Are you, like Mary, afraid of birthing our Savior for this post-modern world? "And the angel [Gabriel] said unto her, '[**NO FEAR**], Mary, for thou hast found favour with God'" (Luke 1:30).

Are you, like Mary Magdalene and the other Mary, afraid that Jesus will abandon you just when you need him most? "And the angel answered and said unto the women, '[**NO FEAR**]: for I know that ye seek Jesus, which was crucified'" (Matt. 28:5 KJV).

Are you afraid, like the shepherds, of a true visitation from God in your ministry? "And the angel said unto them, '[**NO FEAR**]: for, behold, I bring you good tidings of great joy, which shall be to all people'" (Luke 2:10).

Are you afraid, like Paul after his shipwreck, that the wrong turns and shattered wreckage of your life is going to ruin your usefulness for God? "[**NO FEAR**], Paul; thou must be brought before Caesar: and, lo, God hath given thee all them that sail with thee" (Acts 27:24 KJV).

Are you afraid, like Zerubbabel, that God will not complete in you that which God began when God called you into ministry? "According to the promise that I made you when you came out of Egypt. My Spirit abides among you; [**NO FEAR**]" (Hag. 2:5).

Are you afraid, like Israel, of trusting God, afraid of unlearning some things about how God works, afraid of learning new ways of making it to the Promised Land? "[**NO FEAR**], for I am with you, be not dismayed, for I am your God; I will strengthen you, I will help you, I will uphold you with my victorious right hand. . . . For I, the LORD your God, hold your right hand; it is I who say to you, '[**NO FEAR**], I will help you'" (Isa. 41:10, 13).

Are you afraid, like the tribe of Judah, that God has tapped the wrong person, that surely God could find somebody more worthy, more respected, less a joke, to use for this New Reformation into which we are entering? "And as you have been a byword of cursing among the nations, O house of Judah and house of Israel, so will I save you and you shall be a blessing. [**NO FEAR**], but let your hands be strong" (Zech. 8:13).

Are you afraid of the disgrace and discouragement that will come if you follow a new model of ministry? "[**NO FEAR**], for you will not be ashamed; be not confounded, for you will not be put to shame; for you will forget the shame of your youth, and the reproach of your [station] widowhood you will remember no more" (Isa. 54:4).

Are you afraid of becoming a laughingstock, that people are talking about you behind your back and calling you every name in the book? "Hearken to me, you who know righteousness, the people in whose heart is my law; [**FEAR NOT**] the reproach of men, and be not dismayed at their revilings" (Isa. 51:7).

Are you afraid, like Isaac, that God is no longer blessing you, that the wells of living water that you used to draw from have now all gone dry? "And the LORD appeared to him the same night and said, 'I am the God of Abraham your father; [**NO FEAR**], for I am with you and will bless you and multiply your descendants for my servant Abraham's sake'" (Gen. 26:24).

Are you afraid, like Jacob, that the call you heard was so long ago, and so much has happened since then, that it no longer stands? "[**NO FEAR**], nor be afraid; have I not told you from of old and declared it? And you are my witnesses! Is there a God besides me? There is no Rock; I know not any" (Isa. 44:8).

Are you afraid, like Jacob, that God has abandoned you, that you no longer have that anointing from on high? "But now thus says the LORD, he who created you, O Jacob, he who formed you, O Israel: [**NO FEAR**], for I have redeemed you; I have called you by name, you are mine" (Isa. 43:1).

Are you afraid of others' opinions of you? Are you fearful of what people might say if you were to start fishing from the other side of the boat? "Whatsoever this people says, is hard: but [**NO FEAR**] their fear, neither be dismayed" (Isa. 8:12).

Are you afraid of rejection? Are you like Ruth, afraid that you won't be accepted, that your gifts will be rejected, that people will not like you? "Now, my daughter, [**NO FEAR**], I will do to thee all that thou requirest: for all the city of my people doth know that thou art a virtuous woman" (Ruth 3:11 KJV).

Are you afraid that you don't have what it takes to meet the challenges of life and of this new day? "Be strong and of good courage, and do it. [**NO FEAR**], be not dismayed; for the LORD God, even my God, is with you. He will not fail you or forsake you" (1 Chron. 28:20).

Are you afraid, if you're faithful to the gospel, of losing your job? Where would your next payment or bag of groceries come from? "Peace be to you, [**NO FEAR**]: your God, and the God of your father, hath given you treasure in your sacks" (Gen. 43:23 KJV).

Are you afraid of the people in high places who have it in for you and are rooting to see you fail? "[**NO FEAR**] . . . be strong and of good courage: for thus shall the LORD do to all your enemies against whom ye fight" (Josh. 10:25 KJV).

Are you afraid, like the ten spies who saw how gigantic the enemies were that they were facing, that you are little more than a grasshopper? "I said to you, '[**NO FEAR**], be not afraid of them'" (Deut. 1:29).

Are you afraid, like the Israelites, of success, of claiming those promises God has made to you? Are you afraid of what awaits you in the Promised Land? "Behold, the LORD thy God hath set the land before thee: go up and possess it, as the LORD God of thy fathers hath said unto thee; [**NO FEAR**], neither be discouraged" (Deut. 1:21 KJV).

Are you afraid, like the twelve tribes of Israel, of all that wilderness you've got to work your way through before you reach the Promised Land? "[NO FEAR], stand firm, and see the salvation of the LORD, which he will work for you today" (Exo. 14:13).

Are you afraid, like the Christians in Pontus, Galatia, Cappadocia, Asia, and Bithynia, that in this post-Christian future the coming persecution will get worse with every passing year? "Even if you do suffer for righteousness' sake, you will be blessed. Have [NO FEAR] . . . nor be troubled" (1 Pet. 3:14).

Are you afraid, like Saul, that those who are pursuing you will end up with your head? "Dwell with me; [NO FEAR], for wherever I shall seek a place [of safety] for my life, I will also seek a place for thy life, for thou art safely guarded [while] with me" (1 Sam. 23:23).

Are you afraid, like the Psalmist, of fear itself? Are you paranoid? Do you "fear where [NO FEAR] was?" (Ps. 53:5 KJV). "There is [NO FEAR] in love, but perfect love casts out fear; for fear has to do with punishment, and whoever fears has not reached perfection in love" (1 John 4:18 NRSV).

Are you afraid, like the Korahites, of the success of others? Do you fear getting passed by? Does your heart sink a bit when someone else is praised or does something great for God? "[NO FEAR] when a man is enriched, and when the glory of his house in increased" (Ps. 49:16).

Are you afraid, like the Israelites, that God will not forgive you for the awful things you have done? "[NO FEAR] you have done all this evil, yet do not turn aside from following the LORD, but serve the LORD with all your heart" (1 Sam. 12:20).

Are you afraid, like the Israelite army, that you will meet principalities and powers out there that are no match for you? Do the Rushmorean changes that our world is in scare you to death or paralysis? "[NO FEAR]: Let not your hearts faint . . . and do not tremble, neither be ye terrified because of them" (Deut. 20:3 KJV).

Are you afraid, like Joshua, that you don't have the skills to lead your family, your employees, your church into the unknown? Do you fear even the fulfillment of God's promises in your life? "It is [God] that doth go before thee; [God] will be with thee, [God] will not fail thee, neither forsake thee: [**NO FEAR**], neither be dismayed" (Deut. 31:8 KJV).

Are you afraid of being despised for speaking the truth, or mocked for making an ethical decision? "Have [**NO FEAR**] . . . for nothing is covered up that will not be uncovered, and nothing secret that will not become known" (Matt. 10:26 NRSV).

Are you afraid of being persecuted for righteousness sake? "Have [**NO FEAR**] of them which kill the body, but are not able to kill the soul: but rather fear him which is able to destroy both soul and body in hell" (Matt. 10:28 NRSV).

Are you afraid of the future? "[**NO FEAR**], little flock; for it is your Father's good pleasure to give you the kingdom" (Luke 12:32 KJV).

Are you afraid of being let down by God, even forsaken by God after you've put your trust in the Lord? "Why, even the hairs of your head are all numbered. [**NO FEAR**]; you are of more value than many sparrows" (Luke 12:7).

Are you stressed out and anxious, finding it hard to keep off the best-stressed list? "[**NO FEAR**], therefore; you are of more value than many sparrows" (Matt. 10:31).

Are you, like the disciples, afraid when God appears in places and spaces you don't expect him to be, whether wandering on the water or stalking the streets? "Take heart, it is I; [**NO FEAR**]" (Matt. 14:27).

Are you, like Jairus, afraid that God is too late to help your body, your family, your church, your nation? "[**NO FEAR**]: Believe only, and she shall be made whole" (Luke 8:50 KJV).

Are you afraid of the night sky, afraid you can't connect the dots of the thousand points of light God has revealed to you? "[**NO FEAR**], I am the first and the last" (Rev. 1:17).

Are you afraid of being blown away by Pentecost, afraid of what an unleashing and releasing of the power of the risen Christ might do in your life? Jesus says to you as he said to Peter, James, and John: "Jesus came and touched them, saying, 'Rise, and have [**NO FEAR**]'" (Matt. 17:7).

Are you afraid of the success of Spirit-surfing, afraid of the problems of having to haul in full nets that are bursting rather than nets that are barren?

To you Jesus says: "[**NO FEAR**]: from henceforth you shall be netters of men [and women]" (Luke 5:10).

Hezekiah stood before his combat commanders. They were trembling in their boots because the invading army of Sennacherib was about to attack. They were afraid that the challenges of the moment were greater than they were. Hear the words Hezekiah spoke to his leaders of leaders (the same words that Elisha spoke to his servant in 2 Kings 6:16): "Be strong and courageous; [**NO FEAR**] . . . for those who are with us are greater than those who are with them" (2 Chron. 32:7).

Greater is the God that is in you, than any gods that are in the world. When you huff and you puff with the breathings of Pentecost, every house of fear comes tumbling down. Jesus says, "[**NO FEAR**]," God wants to give you the kingdom (Luke 12:32).

N O   F E A R

Chapter 12
THE MYSTERY OF SUFFERING

"Into everyone's life some rain must fall," so the song goes. How many sermons have I preached on what it means to live rain-lashed lives? How many times have I lectured in painstaking detail that every one of us will not get out of life without experiences of suffering, failure, disability, and death? How often have I argued that every one of us needs personal "disasters" to make us, and to make us into the person God intends us to be?

The ultimate measure of a man is not where he stands in moments of comfort and convenience, but where he stands at times of challenge and controversy.

—MARTIN LUTHER KING, JR.

My favorite illustration of this has been the Chevy Chase remake of the classic movie, *The Invisible Man*. Chase becomes invisible after an industrial accident. Henceforth he can only be seen when outlined by rain, powdered concrete, or something that falls on him from above. It's the same way in life: you don't really know the value of a person, or the stuff he's made of, until the rain falls or a bag of powdered concrete drops down from above!

Isn't that when much of the post-modern world begins cursing God? Isn't he the one who brings the rain as well as the sunshine?

I was talking about this subject with environmentalist/gardener Marie Aull one day as we stood at her window watching a spectacular scene outside in her flower bed. At 98, Marie was more observant and open to new discoveries than most people half or a third her age.

At first what we were viewing appeared to be the beginnings of hummingbird wars. One hummer in particular was spending so much time and energy keeping other hummers away from the feeder Marie had set up, he had little time to feed himself. I was appalled! But Marie made me look closer. The hummers that were being driven away were much smaller and wobblier than the one I thought was "protecting" his territory; in fact, they were babies in the midst of a very important lesson. In front of that window was not a hummingbird version of "king-of-the-hill," but a parent who was buzzing its newborns away from the plastic feeder and toward real flowers. Here was a father who did not want any of his children to become dependent on any artificial feeder, no matter how pretty.

Isn't that what's happened to our society? We've become so used to being "fed on demand" through quick fixes (flu shots, anti-aging ointments, Phen-Fen, drive-thru meals, etc.) that we've forgotten it's the hard knocks in life, those character-building moments, that help us make it through with inner peace and joy intact. But how do we regain that perspective in the midst of today's culture? Is there a guiding light?

There was a time and there wasn't a time in the long, long ago (all Arabian folk tales begin this way), when much of the world was unexplored. Map makers had to have some way of portraying unknown areas, so they sometimes dotted these regions with dragons, monsters, and large fish. The message got through: uncharted territories were frightening places. Sailors often feared going too far from shore lest they be gobbled up by sea monsters or fall off the edge of the earth. Terrors lay buried where the dragons appeared. But as every explorer knows, dragons also mark the place of treasures.

One day early in the first century B.C., so the story goes, a commander of a battalion of Roman soldiers was caught up in a battle that took him into territory marked by one of these dragons. Not knowing whether to forge ahead into the unknown or turn back to the familiar (retreat?), he dispatched a messenger to Rome with this urgent request: "Please send new orders. We have marched off the map."

We are now "marching off the map," into the unknown and unwelcome world of suffering and adversity. Though many have suffered before us, each experience is unique and personal, thus creating the sense of aloneness. How are we to navigate, then, in these uncharted waters? Where is the compass to guide us through the storms by day, the North Star to illuminate our path by night?

To answer that question we must struggle with the paradox of Scripture that says both "God is light, and in Him is no darkness at all" (1 John 1:5), and darkness is God's "covering" (Ps. 18:11), God's "dwelling" (1 Kings 8:12), and His "canopy" (2 Sam. 22:12). In Exodus, Moses went into the "thick darkness" to meet God, and in Deuteronomy, God's voice was heard "out of the midst of the darkness." Is it possible that God is the God of the night as well as the God of the light?

It is when things go wrong, when the good things do not happen, when our prayers seem to have been lost, that God is most present. We do not need the sheltering winds when things go smoothly. We are closest to God in the darkness, stumbling along blindly.

—MADELEINE L'ENGLE

And He began to teach them that the Son of Man must suffer many things, and be rejected by the elders and chief priests and scribes, and be killed, and after three days rise again. He spoke this word openly. Then Peter took Him aside and began to rebuke Him. But when He had turned around and looked at His disciples, He rebuked Peter, saying, "Get behind Me, Satan! For you are not mindful of the things of God, but the things of men." When He had called the people to Himself, with His disciples also, He said to them, "Whoever desires to come after Me, let him deny himself, and take up his cross, and follow Me. For whoever desires to save his life will lose it, but whoever loses his life for My sake and the gospel's will save it. For what will it profit a man if he gains the whole world, and loses his own soul? Or what will a man give in exchange for his soul? For whoever is ashamed of me and my words in this adulterous and sinful generation, of him the Son of Man also will be ashamed when He comes in the glory of His Father with the holy angels."

—MARK 8:31–38

The world invites us to climb ladders; the gospel invites us to lift crosses. What will you choose? The ladder or the cross? In the last half-millennium, a work of art that has exerted great symbolic power on a vast number of people is the *Isenheim Altarpiece*, completed in 1515. One art historian has called it a "work of such tremendous and dismal grandeur of expression that nothing on earth seems to equal it." This awesome altarpiece, measuring ten-feet long when closed, twenty-one-feet long when opened, and eight-feet high, is now housed in a museum in Colmar, France. The Order of St. Anthony commissioned the altarpiece for their monastery at Isenheim. They asked Mathias Grunewald—he and Albrecht Durer were considered the greatest artists of the Italian High Renaissance—to present their chapel with something that would bring healing and cleansing to the poor and diseased, something especially for those afflicted with one of the most horrible diseases ever recorded in human history, a disease that wreaked more devastation on the human body than even AIDS—the gangrenous, putrefactive St. Anthony's Fire.

How did the Anthonite monks expect the sick to find healing and cleansing in front of this altarpiece? What kind of therapy was in this painting? The answer was in the successive revelations unveiled by the opening and closing of the altarpiece. When the wings of the altarpiece were closed, the sick and the poor gazed at the crucifixion panel, the most gruesome, tortured, agonized, tormented, almost unbearable crucifixion scene ever painted. There, under a monstrous crown of thorns, was a dangling, pitiful body with twisted limbs, covered with countless lacerations and rivulets of blood. The scene was one of unbearable agony.

When the wings of the altarpiece were opened, however, the dark, deserted landscape and blue-black sky were driven away by a blaze of light. Suddenly, the poor, sick pilgrims stood in awe before three spectacular panels. The first panel contained the most unusual annunciation scene in the world of art; the second depicted the angel choir with seraphs and cherubim celebrating the Virgin and newborn Child; and the third revealed the most glorious resurrection scene ever portrayed, with Jesus exploding from the grave.

In the second panel, the figure of Mary is the Mary of the Magnificat. The angel Gabriel brought Mary a message of authority, not love. To answer the question of your authority as a disciple, your calling as a "minister" of the gospel, you must come to terms with Mary. To be a disciple means you must come to grips with what it must have been like to be Mary, the mother of Jesus. You have heard the angelic call, you have been chosen to receive God's favor. You, the least, the last, the lost, have been called, like Mary, to "give birth" to the Christ child—to bring Christ to your world, to make Christ come alive among men and women in your sphere of influence.

Where was the healing in all this? As Jesus taught in Mark 8, when the life of the cross is entered, authentic life is found. When the body is broken, when blood is poured out, community is born and healing is begun. Pain and suffering open to birth and resurrection. In the words of St. Augustine: "The greater the joy, the greater is the pain which precedes it." Or in the lesson Jesus sought to teach his disciples, before he could reach "the joy set before him," he had to pass through the pain of many dark nights and shadowed valleys. The journey of Jesus' life teaches us, as it taught those with St. Anthony's Fire, that before resurrection sunrise, we must pass through ashes and lashes, spit and spear, thorns and throngs.

You may think you have it together. You may be successful, affluent, well educated, respected. But until you understand the secret behind the Isenheim Altarpiece and why it heals, you are unprepared for being a disciple of Jesus.

There is a popular religious mentality abominating the air today. It says that to find favor with God is to find the perfect boss, the perfect spouse, the perfect child, the perfect colleague, the perfect bishop or pastor, or in the case of pastors, the perfect appointment. (These appointments were known in eighteenth-century circles as the "sweet-scented parishes" because their pastors' salaries were paid in tobacco that was sweeter and more scented and thus more valuable, making clergy vie for transfer to these parishes.) In sum, to find favor is to be blessed by health, wealth, and happiness. This is all that many Americans want in religion. They want a "Jacuzzi Jesus"—an experience that will leave them relaxed, warm, and bubbly and yet, at the same time, feeling fit and trim when they get out—like they've just visited the gym. But the favor of a "Jacuzzi Jesus," the favor of Christian hedonism, is the death of the soul. The favor of a "Jacuzzi Jesus" turns the divine Word being born in you from Logos to logo—from the incarnation of "God's reason" (the literal translation of logos) to the incarnation of the establishment's reason, the logo standards and symbols of the realm religion and temple religion, with all the attendant logos in our culture announcing who is in and who is out.

Some of the great crucifixion scenes in the world of art, from Rogier Van Der Weyden in the fifteenth century, Rembrandt in the seventeenth century, Chagal and Picasso in the twentieth century, do not portray a cross with a ladder propped up against it. A ladder is propped up against the cross only when the artists want to portray Christ's "Descent from the Cross." The ladder was used to take Christ down from the cross, and that is what the ladder symbol does to our churches today—it removes Christ from the cross and from our discipleship.

The gospel shows us, in Paul's words, "a more excellent way." A way not of health, wealth, and happiness, but of servanthood. Mary knew that crucifixion was not a fiction—it was the structuring symbol of her life. She found favor, and ended up pregnant and unmarried. If you, if I, had been the virgin Mary, how many of us would have said "no"? Mary was the first to realize that to accept the gospel is to enter a radically different plausibility structure. The grace of God takes me "just as I am," but the grace of God does not leave us just as we are. It turns our world upside down. The gospel is not the answer. The gospel is the power to become with one another the body of Christ, where the symbol of success is not a golden throne, but a wooden, rugged cross.

There is a very old pulpit story that tells of a customer who went into a jewelry store to buy a cross necklace. The clerk asked: "Do you want to see a plain one? Or do you want to look at the one with a little man on it?"

We want the plain one. We find it difficult to hear the word of the loaded cross, which says that any religious human being encounters suffering, and sees suffering differently. We are hard of hearing when Christ's voice calls us to stay in our suffering even as we become successful and powerful, and calls us to bear always a loaded cross even when we can do more and go farther with a plain one. "Professionalism" has led us to the point where the central motivating symbol of ministry is the ladder rather than the cross.

A conversation with a prospective student who had decided to enter the ministry after a successful, six-figure income career in corporate America illustrates the lethal power resident in the concoction of the careerist-clerical-managerial "ladder" paradigm. "Once I reached the top of the ladder and looked around," he reflected, "I realized that all the struggle, all the costs to my family and friendships, all the sacrifices I had made to reach the pinnacle were not worth what I found there, and the lack of meaning I felt there. Suddenly it hit me: I had propped my ladder up against the wrong building."

Elmer Gantry's pilgrimage from Baptist to Methodist ministry because he wanted to become a bishop immediately comes to mind. Gantry moved up the ladder until the possibility of becoming bishop was in sight, only to discover that by that time, there were more rungs on his career ladder than he realized. A "higher" calling that awakened him to servanthood being the real meaning of his ministry.

The only ladder the Bible knows anything about is Jacob's ladder. Jacob's ladder was pitched against the spiritual, not material. Ladders should always stand in the Garden of Gethsemane and the temple courtyard, not Madison Square Garden and Wall Street. Actually, Jacob had no ladder. He only had a vision and a mission. And he did not climb the ladder, angels did. When the theme song of a disciple becomes "We are climbing Jacob's ladder," then sadly that follower of Jesus has become better at climbing ladders than lifting crosses.

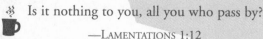 Is it nothing to you, all you who pass by?

—LAMENTATIONS 1:12

Could Herb Caen, the *San Francisco Chronicle* columnist, have been right? He wrote in 1981: "The trouble with born-again Christians is that they are an even bigger pain the second time around."

Conversion without immersion in the life of Jesus Christ is perversion of the gospel. St. Augustine talked about "the costly grace" of God. Discipleship, servanthood, costs us everything. Everything must go. Genesis 2:25 conveys this powerfully in the image of nakedness: "And the man and his wife were both naked, and were not ashamed."

> To be naked means to be without protection; it is to be unarmed. It requires our surrendering the "weapons" that we usually carry around with us. My credit card, my doctorate, the books I have written—the whole fortress in which I live—are all "clothes" that I have to get rid of in order to love.
>
> —DOROTHEE SOELLE

To find favor is to be called to disarmament, called to defenselessness, called to discipleship. God does not favor us with ease. God does not favor us with comfort. One of my favorite signs is posted in an African game reserve: "Advance and be bitten." Paul posted the same sign at the entrance to the Christian life, from Philippians 1:29: "For unto you it is given in the behalf of Christ, not only to believe in him, but also to suffer for his sake." In other words, suffering for the sake of Christ is as much an honor and a blessing as believing in him. The apostles kept the counsel after being beaten, rejoicing that they were "worthy to suffer for his sake."

"Who do you say I am?" Jesus asked, and continues to ask. If your response is, "The Messiah, the Son of the living God!" you are one of God's favored ones. But remember this, your calling as God's favored one cannot promise you success. Your calling as God's favored one cannot promise you prosperity, or popularity, or a life passed only in pleasure. Your calling as God's favored one can only promise you hardship, weariness, suffering, rupture, and. . . .

The *rapture* of "joy unspeakable and full of glory";
The *privilege* of hearing the music of angel choirs;
The *presence* of God who "giveth songs in the night";
The *experience* of walking barefoot on "holy ground";

The *mystery* of discovering the encumbering presence of a love as "strong as death" (Song of Solomon 8:6); and

The *thrill* of spending your life proclaiming to the ashes of dead stars—which is what every human being is made of—these old Welsh words from "Beyond Live and Beckoning Stars":

> Where'er I go the people say,
> "What's the news? What's the news?
> What is the order of the day?
> What's the news? What's the news?"
> Oh, I have got good news to tell.
> My Savior has done all things well.
> He triumphed over death and hell.
> That's the news. That's the news.

That's the good news of the gospel wanting to be born in you—God's terms of endearment, quenching St. Anthony's Fire through you.

Are you ready to say with Mary: "Let it be, to me, according to thy word"? Are you ready to say with Jesus: "Not my will, but thy will be done"? Nothing more. Nothing less. Nothing else.

Are you ready to pray the greatest prayer ever uttered, the simple but great Amen..."So Be It"?

The symbol embodying the most fundamental meaning of discipleship is the cross, not the ladder. We glory in the cross of Christ, not the ladder of success, a ladder kicked away forever when Jesus slipped on the Via Dolorosa.

Remember this: There are no rungs, only nails, on the cross.

Just before Jesus' teaching on suffering to his disciples, he is engages them in conversation, taking them to a place they would never have imagined. They had already witnessed some of the most impressive demonstrations of Jesus' powers: he had fed a crowd of five thousand and another crowd of four thousand on just a few barley loaves and fish; he had walked across water to join his disciples aboard a ship; he had healed a gentile girl who was demon possessed and a man who could neither speak nor hear; he had healed a blind man, fully restoring his vision; on and on the list goes. Surely after all these tremendous acts and signs of power, the disciples felt they were on the road to success. It is not surprising, then, that in response to Jesus' query, "Who do people say that I am?" the disciples didn't even pause for breath before offering three flattering examples of what was blowing in the wind. Obviously the crowds had been talking, and Jesus' disciples had been listening. All three identities the disciples came up with (John the Baptist, Elijah, one of the prophets) represented powerful, God-inspired voices. With his next question, however, Jesus puts his disciples on the spot: "But who do you say that I am?" Now Jesus was asking for their conclusions to what they had seen and heard.

It is the outspoken Peter who is the first to offer up an answer. The name, "Christos," which Peter declares may be variously translated as "the Christ," "the Messiah" or "the Anointed One." Christos, however, is not used here as a proper name, it's a job description. "You are the one who performs miracles, sets all things right, alleviates pain and suffering. You are the one who makes feeding the family easy." What a shocker when Jesus immediately begins to offer his disciples his own version of messiahship, that of suffering and eventual death. Immediately Peter vehemently argues with Jesus, claiming such cannot be the case! What he had missed in his Master's description of Christhood was the punchline: he would rise again. As the Christ, Jesus would "undergo great suffering, even death," but he would also "rise again." Wouldn't it have changed the picture if only the disciples had asked what Jesus meant by that?

But now the disciples' private lesson was over; Jesus turned to include the crowd in his next address. For those who had not heard his private prediction of his own suffering, death, and resurrection, these words must have shocked the crowd right down to their sandals. For Jesus lays out requirements for discipleship that go far beyond any usual conversion practices. In those days, Jewish proselytes had to freely accept Jewish faith and law, including circumcision, and willingly reject old pagan relationships and acquaintances. But Jesus' insistence that a potential disciple must not only deny all old familiar ties but must be prepared to suffer horrible atrocities because of their identity as a disciple was unprecedented.

After two millennia of "cross" imagery, our senses are not as shocked by this reference as Jesus' listeners must have been. The pain, brutality, and degradation of a death by crucifixion—including the spirit-stripping practice of making the condemned take up his own cross on the final death march to the execution site—was a torture reserved for only the most despised of state criminals. Yet this is the very image Jesus chooses to represent as the fate of his most devoted disciples.

As evidence that cross-bearing must become the true disciple's way, Jesus offers his listeners the paradox of Mark 8:35. The "life" saved or lost is the Greek "psyche," which includes a threefold dimension: "life," "soul," and "oneself." Clearly, all three meanings are intended by Jesus' declaration. The blatant expression of physical cost has already been highlighted by references to suffering and the focus on the cross, a device of physical torture. But here there is an additional sense of "life" as well. A sense of individual identity, of "oneself" and the unique "soul" that animates every living person, is part of the natural desire for self-preservation that Jesus turns topsy-turvy with his words. Jesus' rhetorical question, "What can they give in return for their life?" leads his listeners to the conclusion that only "life itself" can be offered as an adequate response to the gift of life. For both the disciples and the crowds who had up to this point been enjoying a journey of triumph and miracles, Jesus' new message was both sobering and hard to swallow.

Today the cost of discipleship is still sobering and hard to swallow; many chose an easier way. The final comment offered by Jesus, "For whoever is ashamed of me and my words in this adulterous and sinful generation, of him the Son of Man also will be ashamed when He comes in the glory of His Father with the holy angels," reminds his listeners—and us—that whatever choice they make, for Jesus or against him, there will be eternal consequences.

The cross is the exhibition of the nature of God, the gateway whereby any individual of the human race can enter into union with God. When we get to the cross, we do not go through it; we abide in the life to which the cross is the gateway.

—OSWALD CHAMBERS

Let me learn, O God, that my
tears as well as my words
may reach your heart and be
regarded by you as genuine prayer. . . .
Just as without the rain
there can be no rainbow,
so also eyes that never weep
can never glow with sympathy and gentleness.
Give me, Lord, evermore a tender
as well as a pure, heart.

—ADAPTED FROM JOHN CALVIN REID

Chapter 13
TRUSTING GOD'S FAITHFULNESS

There is no song so broken, no monotone so horrible, no voice so tremulous, that God can't take it and compose it into a beautiful symphony.

Have you ever played the game "Gossip" or "Rumors"? After gathering everyone into a circle, one person begins by whispering some message to his neighbor, softly and quietly. The neighbor must then pass along that whispered message (or at least the version he or she heard of it) to the person sitting on the other side. Everyone gets only one chance to hear what is said before telling it to the next one in the circle. It's not hard to imagine how scrambled, or even unrecognizable, the original message can be once it comes back, full circle, to the ear of the leader.

Despite the advent of high-tech communication—E-mail, faxes, conference calls—a lot of messages and stories still seem to get through our culture on the old gossip chain. Typically, these stories are altered and adjusted to fit the part of the country they emerge from, the economic status of the community, or the local prides and prejudices. Some cultural rumor-stories have been around for decades. Ever hear about the snake in the coat at Kmart, or was it a python living on a sale table at Wal-Mart or a boa constrictor found under the collar of a mink coat in a Manhattan boutique? The periodic resurgence of this story must be trying to tell us something about our culture.

Recently another story has been working its way through a kind of underground rumor mill. It, too, reveals something about the desires and fears of post-modern life. When first heard, this story seemed too amazing to be true. It had all the earmarks of a "snake-in-the-Kmart" rumor. But the tale has persisted, and we have finally tracked it down to its source. The following truly happened and involved a definite time, place, and person.

This story is about the impact the faith of one nameless, homeless street person has had on people more than 25 years after his death. Tapes of this homeless person have been played in homeless shelters all across America. Thanks to the grinding of the rumor mill, this homeless person has erroneously been located in such diverse places as Miami's 7th Street and 1st Avenue, New York City's 54th and Lexington, and on the street corners of other lonely, urban centers. Also in various versions of this tale, the homeless person has "mysteriously" disappeared, suggesting to a hopeful culture that he was actually some sort of angel-in-residence. It is both reassuring and remarkable that when the genuine story was finally tracked down, it was as moving and miraculous as any of the gossiped versions that had been circulating across the globe.

The story involves Gavin Bryars, England's leading musician/composer. In 1971, Bryars agreed to help his friend Alan Powers with the audio aspects of a film Powers was making about street people. The filming took place in an area around London's Waterloo Station. Powers filmed various people living on the streets, catching with the camera's eye their daily rituals, trials, and joys. Some were obviously drunk, some mentally disturbed, some articulate, some apparently incomprehensible. As Bryars made his way through the audio and video footage, he became aware of a constant undercurrent, a repeating sound that always accompanied the presence of one older man. At first the sound seemed like muttered gibberish. But after removing the background street noise and cleaning up the audio tape, Bryars discovered the old man was in fact singing.

Ironically, the footage of this old man and his muttered song didn't "make the cut." But the filmmaker's loss was Bryars' gain. He took the rejected audio tape and could not escape the haunting sounds of this homeless, nameless man. So he did some research on his own into who this homeless person might be. From the film crew, Bryars learned that this street beggar did not drink, but neither did he engage others in conversation. His speech was almost impossible to understand, but his demeanor was sunny. Though old and alone, filthy and homeless, he retained a certain playfulness. For example, he took delight in teasingly swapping hats with various members of the film crew. But what distinguished this old man from other street people was his song. The song he sang under his breath was a simple, repetitive Sunday school tune, but for him it was a mantra. He would sit and quietly sing it, uninterrupted, for hours on end:

> Jesus' blood never failed me yet Never failed me yet Jesus' blood never failed me yet There's one thing I know For he loves me so. . . .

Like a film loop, the song's final line fed into its first line, starting the tune over and over and over again without ceasing. The man's weak, old, untrained voice never wavered from pitch, never went flat, never changed key. The simple intervals of the tune were perfectly maintained for however long he sang. As a musician, Bryars was fascinated. He began thinking of ways he could arrange and orchestrate around the constant, repeated lines the old man sang.

One day, while playing the tape as background to other work, Bryars left the door to his studio open while he ran downstairs to get a cup of coffee. When he returned several minutes later, he found a normally buzzing office environment eerily stilled. The old man's quiet, quavery voice had leaked out of the recording room and transformed the office floor. Under the spell of this stranger's voice, an office of busy professionals had grown hushed. Those who were still moving around walked slowly, almost reverently about the room. Many more had taken their seats and were sitting motionless at their desks, transfixed by the voice. More than a few were silently weeping, tears cascading undisturbed down their faces.

Bryars was stunned. Although not a believer himself, he could not help but be confronted by the mysterious spiritual power of this unadorned voice. Sitting in the midst of an urban wilderness, this John-the-Baptist voice touched a lonely, aching place that lurks in the human heart, offering an unexpected message of faith and hope in the midst of the darkest, most blighted night.

Soon Bryars himself started yearning for the confidence and faith this old man's song celebrates. He began to face what it means to feel homeless and alone even when we are sitting in the midst of our families. He vowed to respect this homeless person by creating a recording that would celebrate and accentuate his simple message, that no matter what one's condition, Jesus "loves me so. . . ."

It took England's leading contemporary composer until 1993 to create and produce what he felt was a proper accompaniment to this homeless person's song of trust and obedience. This he did in partnership with one of America's leading composers, Philip Glass. Glass, who is probably best known for his work "Koyaanisquatsi," (the title, translated from Hopi, means "Life out of Balance") brought his musical mixture of rock realism and mysticism to the project. The result is a CD entitled "Jesus' Blood Never Failed Me Yet," from Mneumonic (1993). The old man died shortly after that film crew left his street-home. It was almost as if, when someone finally heard his song, he could leave for another place. Who knows? Maybe he was an angel after all.

What convinced these leading musicians/composers to create a musical framework to preserve this old man's song? Why did an office full of busy people find themselves reduced to tears at the sound of his voice? How did this tiny scrap of audiotape from the cutting room floor ever survive to live on for thousands to hear?

Each one of us has a broken song, a quivery voice, a frail pitch. But the Advent message is that one homeless night long ago, in a place called Bethlehem, God wrapped humanity's broken songs and shattered chords with the music of the spheres. Through the birth of Jesus of Nazareth, God gave each of our feeble attempts at singing a cosmic orchestra of surround-sound spirituality. That Christmas night, our scratchy, scruffy voices were lifted forever to the skies.

As is often the case, God is most attentive when God seems most absent. For many Jews, there was no darker time—a time when God seemed more silent—than the time of the Roman occupancy in Israel. The prophets' words had come true, and now there was nothing but silence from God's chosen people, to God's chosen people.

Yet in the coming of Christ, God was faithful. Faithfulness is one of the defining attributes of God. For Paul, the faithfulness of God was inextricably caught up in the righteousness of God. If God was truly righteous, then God must be unequivocally faithful. The righteousness of God, in fact, is an expression of God's faithfulness to God's own self. Without faithfulness, the righteousness of God cannot participate in redemptive activity.

God's providence is also bound up in God's faithfulness—for a providential God to work out the divine plans according to the divine Will requires unswerving faithfulness. The classic Calvinist understanding of divine providence insists that God's constant, providential governance of all that occurs directs creation toward a preordained end. Unless God is faithful to this providential trajectory, Calvin rightly insisted, all creation moves along on its own accord.

In 1925, the *New York World* celebrated the birthday of Abraham Lincoln with a cartoon which has become something of a classic. Two Kentucky farmers are pictured, talking over a picket fence. One asks, "Anything new happen lately?" The other responds, "Nothing much. A new baby was born over at Tom Lincoln's place, but nothing much ever happens around here." I'm sure there were folks who said the same thing in Bethlehem that night. I can picture them, can't you? Standing on the corner, just outside the inn. "Anything new happen around here?" "Naw, just a baby born down in the stable. Nothing much ever happens around here."

—JAMES A. HARNISH

In my discipleship I will be—like David, lifting up mine eyes unto the hills from whence comes my help; like Paul, forgetting those things which are behind and pressing on forward; like Abraham, trusting completely in our God; like Sarah, laughing for joy at God's great promise; like Enoch, walking in daily fellowship with our Creator; like Moses, choosing life over death; like Jehoshaphat, preparing my heart to seek God; like Mary, loving God so much she birthed our Lord and Savior; like Daniel, able to commune with God all the time; like Job, patient under all circumstances; like Ruth, loyal above all to family; like Caleb and Joshua, refusing to be discouraged even in the face of greater numbers; like Joseph, able to turn away from all evil advances; like Gideon, advancing even though friends be few; like Aaron and Hur, constantly upholding the hands of our spiritual leaders; like Isaiah, consecrated to always do God's work; like John, leaning upon the example of the Master Teacher; like Andrew, ever striving to lead my family to a closer walk with Christ; like Priscilla, a pioneer for growing churches; like Stephen, manifesting a forgiving spirit toward all people; like the angels, proclaiming the message of peace and good will to all.

In my discipleship, I will be such!

—WESLEY D. TAYLOR

When the signs of age begin to mark my body (and still more when they touch my mind); when the ill that is to diminish me or carry me off strikes from without or is born within me; when the painful moment comes in which I suddenly awaken to the fact that I am ill or growing old; and above all at that last moment when I feel I am losing hold of myself and am absolutely passive within the hands of the great unknown forces that have formed me; in all those dark moments, O God, grant that I may understand that it is you . . . who are painfully parting the fibers of my being in order to penetrate to the very marrow of my substance and bear me away within yourself. . . . It is not enough that I should die while communicating. Teach me to communicate while dying.

—THE DIVINE MILIEU

A 1996 AT&T TV commercial starred Dick Cavett observing that "There isn't much you can count on these days." Then comes the punchline: "But you can count on AT&T."

Hello?!?

Some of you reading these words are probably part of the forty thousand "laid off" by AT&T very soon after that ad came out. No one knows more than you what it is to feel like "there isn't much you can count on these days."

Who can you count on anymore? Who can you trust? We are living in a world where trust is one of our most endangered virtues and values. In the midst of the world's trust crisis, to a people suffering a trust deficit, it is time to announce at the top of our lungs, "In God We Trust!"

 Blessed is the one who trusts in the Lord, whose trust is the Lord.

—JEREMIAH 17:7

When I am afraid, I will trust in you.

—PSALM 56:3

 Taste and see that the Lord is good. Blessed is the one that trusts in God.

—PSALM 34:8

 You will keep in perfect peace whose mind is steadfast,
because they trust in you.

—ISAIAH 26:3

 Cast all your anxiety on God because God cares for you.

—I PETER 5:7

Alas, instead of reminding this now low-trust nation of its high-trust motto, one hears from church folk what one hears from everyone else: "In Ourselves We Trust." Paradoxically, the more we trust ourselves above God, and the more we strive to become sovereigns of our own life, the more obsessed we become with issues of control.

Nineties culture is fixated on control. We've become control freaks, control junkies, control addicts. Our churches are no different. They are jam-packed with people playing control games. How ironic that some of the leading lights of post-modern culture are denouncing the way in which our need for control is itself out of control, and has become an addiction. Kevin Kelley of *Wired* magazine has written a book inviting those who would live in the twenty-first century to inhabit a future of chaos, complexity, and uncertainty by going "out of control," a phrase that he asks us to hear as positive. Those who will let go and let science, technology, and evolution have their way, Kelley argues, can expect to thrive in the twenty-first century.

John Wesley, who was out of control before out of control was cool, announced to the Enlightenment world that the only one worth trusting is God. He wrote an out-of-control covenant, which he recited for forty years as part of his New Year's Eve Watch Night service, that went like this:

> I am no longer my own,
> but yours.
> Put me to what You will,
> rank me with whoever you will.
> Put me to doing . . .
> Put me to suffering.
> Let me be employed for You,
> or laid aside for You.
> Exalted for You, or
> Brought low for You.
> Let me be full
> Let me be empty
> Let me have all things,
> Let me have nothing!
> And now, O Father,
> You are mine and I am Yours.
> So be it. And the covenant I am
> making on earth,
> Let it be ratified in heaven.
> Amen.

Since then other out-of-control disciples have written their own confessionals, from the one attributed to a "young Asian underground pastor" who taped on the wall of his house in Beijing, China, a declaration that he was a part of "The Fellowship Committed to Doing Whatever It Takes," to the late musician Keith Green's song of promise, "Pledge My Head to Heaven," that goes like this:

> Well I pledge my head to heaven for the Gospel
> And I ask no man on earth to fill my needs,
> Like the sparrow of the boat, I am enveloped in His love,
> And I trust Him like those little ones He feeds.
> Well I pledge my wife to heaven for the Gospel
> Though our love each passing day just seems to grow,
> As I told her when we wed, I'd surely rather be found dead
> Than to love her more than the One who saved my soul.
> Well I pledge my son to heaven for the Gospel
> Though he's kicked and beaten, ridiculed and scorned,
> I will teach him to rejoice and lift a thankful, praising voice
> And to be like Him who bore the nails and crown of thorns.
> I'm your child, and I wanna be in your family forever!
> I'm your child, and I'm gonna follow you no matter whatever the cost,
> I'm going to count all things lost.
> Well I've had the chance to gain the world and live just like a king,
> But without your love it doesn't mean a thing!
> I pledge my son, I pledge my wife,
> I pledge my head to heaven for the Gospel.

In a similar spirit, I have written my own post-modern confession of faith. I call it my "Magna Carta of Trust." Like a cross placed in front of Dracula, I place this confession in front of this Oklahoma-City-bombing ridden, Wall Street driven, Disneyland-bidden culture and all of its violent visions, sadisms of the spirit, and tin-eared trendinitis. I also place this confession in front of a church jam-packed with Christian agnostics—professionally religious men and women with too little personal faith in, and relationship with, Jesus of Nazareth to let go and let God. It goes like this:

I am part of the Church of the Out-of-Control. I once was a control junkie, but now am an out-of-control disciple. I've given up my control to God. I trust and obey the Spirit. I've jumped off the fence; I've stepped over the line; I've pulled out all the stops; I'm holding nothing back. There's no turning back, looking around, slowing down, backing away, letting up, or shutting up. It's a life against the odds, outside the box, over the wall, the game of life played without goal lines other than "Thy Will be Done. . . ."

I'm done lap-dogging the topdogs, the wonderdogs, the overdogs, or even the underdogs. I'm done playing according to the rules, whether its Robert's Rules of Order or Miss Manner's Rules of Etiquette or Martha Stewart's Rules of Living or Louis Farrakhan's Rules of America's Least Wanted or Merrill Lynch's Money-minding/Bottom-lining/Ladder-climbing Rules of America's Most Wanted.

I am not here to please the dominant culture or to serve any all-show, no-go bureaucracies. I live to please my Lord and Savior. My spiritual taste buds have graduated from fizz and froth to Fire and Ice. Sometimes I'm called to sharpen the cutting edge, and sometimes to blunt the cutting edge. Don't give me that old-time religion. Don't give me that new-time religion. Give me that all-time religion that's as hard as rock and as soft as snow.

I've stopped trying to make life work, and started trying to make life sing. I'm finished with secondhand sensations; third-rate dreams; low-risk, high-rise trades; and goose-stepping, flag-waving crusades. I no longer live by and for anything but everything God-breathed, Christ-centered, and Spirit-driven.

I can't be bought by any personalities or perks, positions or prizes. I won't give up, though I will give in . . . to openness of mind, humbleness of heart, and generosity of spirit. When shorthanded and hard-pressed, I will never again hang in there. I will stand in there; I will run in there; I will pray in there; I will sacrifice in there; I will endure in there—in fact I will do everything in there but hang. My face is upward; my feet are forward; my eyes are focused; my way is cloudy; my knees are worn; my seat, uncreased; my heart, burdened; my spirit, light; my road, narrow; my mission, wide.

I won't be seduced by popularity, traduced by criticism, travestied by hypocrisy, or trivialized by mediocrity. I am organized religion's best friend and worst nightmare. I won't back down, slow down, shut down, or let down until I'm preached out, teached out, healed out, or hauled out of God's mission in the world entrusted to members of the Church of the Out-of-Control . . . to unbind the confined, whether they're the down-trodden or the upscale, the overlooked or the under-represented.

My fundamental identity is as a disciple of Jesu—but even more, as a disciple of Jesus who lives in Christ, who doesn't walk through history simply "in His steps," but seeks to travel more deeply in His Spirit.

Until He comes again or calls me home, you can find me filling, not killing, time so that one day He will pick me out in the line-up of the ages as one of His own. And then . . . it will be worth it all . . . to hear these words, the most precious words I can ever hear: "Well done, thou good and faithful . . . Out-of-Control Disciple."

I challenge you to draw up your own credo of trust. Be it short or long—one phrase or an entire book—let it get to the heart of your fear and desire for control, and draw you to a confidence in the God Who Can.

Trust Him when dark doubts assail thee,
Trust him when your faith is small,
Trust him when simply to trust him
is the hardest thing of all.

—POEM FOUND IN ROSALIND RUSSELL'S PRAYER BOOK

AFTER HER DEATH IN 1976

Chapter 14
SPIRITUAL HEIRLOOMS

It used to be that when we took a family member or visitor to the airport, there was plenty of time for formal, cordial good-byes. Saying goodbye was an art. You had to work up to a high point, a final message, a last hug, at just the right time. Too soon and you would have to endure those last minutes knowing everything had already been said. Too late and you would end up shouting crucial messages at someone's back down the jetway. Timing was everything. Curbside check-in has changed everything. Now there is rarely time to get the traveler and his or her luggage out of the car before other vehicles are honking at you for blocking traffic. You can't craft a meaningful, heartfelt farewell while trying to get a garment bag out of your trunk, handing tickets to a skycap, and worrying about that next car in line pinning you to the bumper. Our "good-byes" have become something we simply shout out from across the driver's side of the car, over the roar of traffic and the smell of exhaust.

What a pity. Because good-byes are messages that can stay with us. Leaving family or friends is a poignant, sometimes painful moment in our lives. We tend consciously to remember all the details of our final minutes together. As children, we all experienced a very important good-bye every day of our lives—when we were tucked into bed and left alone in the dark. Our parents called it "good night," but this end-of-the-day ritual is really a good-bye, a farewell to the day we shared together.

Do you remember the last words your parents spoke to you before you went to bed at night? Did it vary from night to night or did you have a set routine? What is the last thing you say to your kids before they go to bed? Susan Goodwin Stiles, of Foley, Minnesota, has two little girls—ages 6 and 4. As she tucks her daughters into bed each night, Susan recites a special mantra to them, "Remember, you are special to God. Remember how much we love you. Sleep loose."

Hello! Sleep loose? The Stiles recite this strange-sounding directive to their girls each night for a very important reason: they want their children to relax and let go to the love of God that surrounds each of them. They want their children to sleep loose in the security of that divine love. Too many children, too many adults, are sleeping "tight" instead—tensed and ready to bolt and run at the slightest appearance of danger, the smallest indication of risk. It is hard to get a good night's rest when all of your muscles are taut. Sleeping tight is an uncomfortable, unhappy way to go through life. But for those who know they are "special," that they are "loved," each bedtime brings the comfort and security of sleeping loose.

> Finally, brothers, good-bye. Aim for perfection, listen to my appeal, be of one mind, live in peace. And the God of love and peace will be with you. Greet one another with a holy kiss. All the saints send their greetings. May the grace of the Lord Jesus Christ, and the love of God, and the fellowship of the Holy Spirit, be with you all.
>
> —2 CORINTHIANS 13:11–14

These words, Paul's last to the Corinthians, demonstrate how a well-crafted goodbye can be meaningful and moving. Paul's future, as well as the future of the Corinthian Christians, was unclear. The apostle continued to face the possibilities of persecution, arrest, and execution. The Corinthian church had both its internal battles and the external threats of persecution to cloud its destiny. When Paul invokes his message of "farewell" to these Christians, it reaches beyond the moment of its reading.

Farewell also means may you have a good journey, and the journey Paul constantly envisioned is one that travels through this life toward an ultimate destination with God. Paul's good-bye to the Corinthians, then, is like his spiritual "triptych" for their own journey through life, even unto death. The words Paul left ringing in their ears offered the Corinthians a prescription for holy living—a way to sleep loose every night of their lives.

1. Put things in order. This is Paul's attempt to get the Corinthians to prioritize. When we put our lives in proper order, "last things" (the things that "last") will go "first." That which is important will separate out from the extraneous "junk" we find cluttering up our lives. We can't sleep loose if our beds are hidden under piles of this junk.

2. Listen to my appeal. The most important word here is listen. We can't hear if we won't be quiet and tune in. Listening saves us from the risk of going off half-cocked, misinformed, and misdirected. To sleep loose, we must listen for the message of God's love, which comes to us through the sounds of the Holy Spirit.

3. Agree with one another. We are not just to tolerate each other's company (some of the Corinthians apparently could not even do that). We are called to celebrate one another. Since God's love extends to each of us, there is reason to celebrate every individual. Instead of criticizing shortcomings and highlighting the negatives of each other, try emphasizing the positives. Just because we have differences doesn't mean we can't agree to disagree in love.

4. Live in peace. When differences are celebrated instead of castigated, we can experience harmony instead of discord, shalom

instead of shouting. Sleeping loose takes place in such peace and quiet.

5. Receive the gift of love. Susan Stiles's four- and six-year-old daughters are probably better at receiving love than most of us are. Children receive love graciously and un-self-consciously. For adults, it is more difficult to relax and sleep loose in the offer of God's love after we have spent the day keeping our vulnerabilities tightly locked away from view. We can accept that God is love, but it is far more difficult to accept that God is love for us. The joy and bliss of the Holy Spirit is ours.

6. Join the cloud of witnesses. Paul invoked the presence of "all the saints" in his farewell to the Corinthians. Likewise, we must feel a part of all the saints, the entire community of faith. It is in feeling the strength of all that support that we can relax and sleep loose.

What kind of good-bye do you plan on giving to your family and friends?

In the summer of 1993, my brothers and I became orphans. My mother, Mabel Boggs Sweet, who had spent the last years of her life with me, died on July 20 of that year. She was 81. My father, Leonard Lucius Sweet, died twenty-one years before at the age of 57, one week before I was to graduate from seminary. The first funeral service I ever officiated, as a priest, was my father's.

My mother was the dominant spiritual and educational influence of my life. So what seemed at first a minor question for us three boys—"What kind of tombstone shall we get Mom and Dad?"—turned into a major issue that each of us answered differently. In the selection of a gravestone, we wanted to show the respect and love we felt for our parents. We almost hired one of those new "cemetery artists" who contract with families to sculpt in stone highly personalized monuments that feature the values and uniqueness of loved ones. But before we supported with mega bucks this newly burgeoning industry of cemetery art, which harkens back to those majestic Egyptian sarcophagi and elaborate Victorian memorials, we decided to take a different route.

A very dignified but simple gravestone marks our parents' burial site in upstate New York. The real tombstone, which says what my brothers and I really wanted to say about our love for our parents, is found in each one of our homes. We spent our money, not on something we would visit once a year, but on something we would live with every day.

My mother's tombstone is an ornately decorated piano, that occupies with pride a special place in my living room. Why a piano for a tombstone? Mother followed to the letter the Susannah Wesley manual in child rearing. We had family devotions twice a day—first thing in the morning and the last thing at night. After getting up from our knees, Mother would usher me, Phil, and John upstairs, tuck us in our respective beds, kiss us good night, and then return downstairs where she would immediately sit down at our old upright piano. Mother didn't read us books in bed; our nighttime stories were Bible stories read in the devotional circle, as often by us boys as by our parents. Our bedside ritual was shouting downstairs our requests of what we wanted her to sing while she played the piano. Mother then lulled us to sleep singing the hymns of the faith. As the eldest son, and stubbornest, I refused to be lullabyed to sleep until I had gotten in the last request—the beginning of a lifelong habit, I'm afraid.

Over the course of the years, that old piano did not find its way to Mother and Dad's final home. So when I heard about a late eighteenth century upright German piano—made by J. Doll and Kamprath of Hamburg—going on the auction block in Chattanooga, Tennessee, I knew instantly what my mother's tombstone would be. The carved eagle that hovers over the keyboard is the symbol of John's Gospel, Mother's favorite. (I too have come to believe that one of the greatest writers in the history of the world is St. John the Evangelist.) The birds flanking the sides, and the dog-legged piano base were almost too good to be true—we always had pet birds and dogs in our home. The piano needs some internal repair and constant tuning, but every time I play it, I am reminded how my own life needs a lot of interior repair and tuning, and how my mother was a tool in the hand of God to carve me into who I am today.

My main tuner in life, Mother, is physically missing, and the whole world seems "depopulated" (as Lamartine said it would, under these circumstances). But Mother has become for me the "living dead." Her spirit is still alive and present in my life, and this tombstone serves as her daily reminder to me to tune my life to God's perfect pitch, Jesus the Christ, God's tuning fork to the eternal. The tombstone's dedicatory verse is this admonition St. Paul gave to his friend and colleague, Timothy: "Keep safe what has been entrusted to you" (1 Tim. 6:20).

There is a book on epitaphs worthy of the subject. By Nigel Rees, the book is called Epitaphs: A Dictionary of Grave Epigrams and Memorial Eloquence. It shares what family and friends thought of some people, and in a few cases, what others thought of themselves. Here are a few of them:

Following is what the family and friends of Howard Ashman, songwriter for Disney's Beauty and the Beast and The Little Mermaid, engraved on his tombstone when he died of AIDS in 1991:

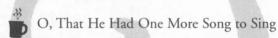 O, That He Had One More Song to Sing

There are epitaphs written for famous people by others, like this one E.V. Lucas composed for G.K. Chesterton:

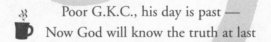 Poor G.K.C., his day is past —
Now God will know the truth at last

I love the way our forbearers told the truth in death as well as in life:

Here lies the body of Mary Anne
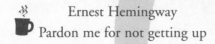 Safe in the arms of Abraham.
All very well for Mary Anne
But how about poor Abraham?

Here's one written by a famous person for himself:

Ernest Hemingway
Pardon me for not getting up

This was much better in its original form on the tombstone of a man named Yeast:

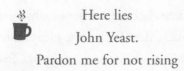

Here lies
John Yeast.
Pardon me for not rising

What pastor doesn't know exactly what Will Smith went through in life when on his tombstone one reads:

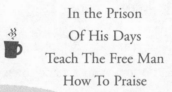

Here lies
Will Smith —
and, what's something rarish,
He was born, bred, and hanged,
all in the same parish

My two favorites in the collection?

One is found on the memorial slab to W.H. Auden in Poets' Corner, Westminster Abbey:

In the Prison
Of His Days
Teach The Free Man
How To Praise

The other, President Harry S Truman said he found in Boot Hill Cemetery in Tombstone, Arizona. He said it was the "greatest epitaph a man could have":

Here lies
Jack Williams.
He done
his damnedest

How will your life be reflected in the epitaph on your tombstone? Do you think this is not a question for you to ponder, only leave up to those who survive you? Think again. The life we lead now, and the fervor with which we live it and pass it on to others, will directly influence what others write about us in death.

One of the best short essays I've read was one by Robert Noel Test. With only a high school education, Test felt so impassioned about the meaning of his life that one day, on his lunch break, he penned "To Remember Me":

"The day will come when my body will lie upon a white sheet, neatly tucked under four corners of a mattress located in a hospital busily occupied with the living and the dying. At a certain moment, a doctor will determine that my brain has ceased to function and that, for all intents and purposes, my life has stopped.

"When that happens, do not attempt to instill artificial life into my body by the use of a machine. And don't call this my 'deathbed.' Call it my 'bed of life,' and let my body be taken from it to help others lead fuller lives.

"Give my sight to someone who has never seen a sunrise, a baby's face or love in the eyes of a woman.

"Give my heart to a person whose own heart has caused nothing but endless days of pain.

"Give my blood to the teenager who has been pulled from the wreckage of his car, so that he might live to see his grandchildren play.

"Give my kidneys to one who depends on a machine to exist from week to week.

"Take my bones, every muscle, every fiber and nerve in my body and find a way to make a crippled child walk.

"Explore every corner of my brain. Take my cells, if necessary, and let them grow so that someday a speechless boy will shout at the crack of a bat and a deaf girl will hear the sound of rain against her window.

"Burn what is left of me and scatter the ashes to the winds to help the flowers grow.

"If you must bury something, let it be my faults, my weaknesses and all my prejudices against my other humans.

"Give my sins to the devil.

"Give my soul to God.

"If, by chance, you wish to remember me, do it with a kind deed or word to someone who needs you. If you do all I have asked, I will live forever."

What have you given others to remember you by? How will your life effectively change the lives of those who survive you? What will your spiritual heirloom be?

Generally speaking, the "Middle Ages" or "Dark Ages" —those centuries after the Roman Empire fell and before Europe established itself as the new center for intellectual and cultural richness—are remembered for their cold weather, bad food and nonexistent plumbing. But there was one bright spot in the darkness, where medieval men and women gathered from miles around for comfort and Christian training: the cathedral. It is here that these so-called Dark Ages continue to shine their brightest light, for through the media of stained-glass windows, primitive sculptures and icons, paintings and murals, the local cathedral became effectively one massive, open Bible. Though our medieval forbearers did not have the Bible in book form, the Biblical stories told through cathedral art gave them a deep, rich understanding of the Christian faith.

God wants us to be like cathedral art, the stained glass that sheds his light on the world around us. Keith Green, wrote his own version of this in his song, "Stained Glass," taken from Matthew 5:16: "Let your light so shine before men, that they may see your good works, and glorify your Father which is in heaven."

We are like windows
Stained with colors
Of the rainbow
Set in a darkened room
'Til the Bridegroom
Comes to shine Thru.
Then the colors fall around our feet
Over those we meet
Coloring all the gray that we see,
Rainbow colors of assorted hues
Come exchange your blues
For His love that you see shining
thru me.

Modeling or "mentoring" is a popular concept today. But what does it mean for you and me to be model/mentor Christians? Although mentors or teachers often appear in elevated or "up-front" positions, genuine mentors do not try to be stars. Rather, the role of the Christian mentor is that of a lamp to illumine the pathway that lies directly at his or her student's feet, offering guidance and service in indirect ways.

Even after death, your lamp still burns; and there are no lamps that cannot throw at least a little light on some darkened portion of a fellow traveler's pathway. Take confidence now in the potential power of your lamp—in the present and for the future—for its light source is truly unquenchable.

A story I heard once illustrates this well. I went to a leadership seminar where one of the speakers, author and chaplain Ben Patterson, told about his spiritual heirloom to his children.

"I work my Bible to shreds about every five years," Ben shared, "so when we had our first child I decided to dedicate my new Bible to him. I am now working on my third Bible like this.

"Before I open my Bible to do my devotions, or exegete certain passages, I pray for the child for whom this Bible is dedicated. While I am working through the Scriptures I write notes to him in the margins, telling him how much this verse means to me or informing him of a prayer I offered for him while reading that text.

"Sometimes I find a poem I want to share with him and stuff it in the pages. Or sometimes a quote will come to mind, or a special wish for him, and I jot that down, too. Then, when my Bible is so threadbare and worn from working through it and preaching from it and taking it with me everywhere I go, I present it to him on his birthday as a special gift from his father."

What spiritual heirlooms are you and I bequeathing to our children, our neighbors, our church, our community, our world?

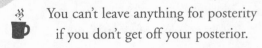

You can't leave anything for posterity
if you don't get off your posterior.